JAY HARRINGTON

THE PRODUCTIVITY
P1VOT

Build a Profitable Legal Practice

By Selling Yourself One Hour

Every Day

ORDERING INFORMATION

For additional copies visit www.hcommunications.biz/books, www.attorneyatwork.com/books, or www.amazon.com. Quantity discounts available—for more information visit www.productivitypivot.com or email the author at jay@hcommunications.biz.

ISBN
978-0-9995545-5-5

For more information, and free resources related to the book, visit **www.productivitypivot.com**.

TABLE OF CONTENTS

—

Introduction

"Time is what we want most,
but use worst."
– WILLIAM PENN

You have the potential to accomplish what most lawyers fail to do, which is to build an empowering and profitable legal practice. Whether you're at a large law firm or a small one, there are opportunities for you to attract and engage with new clients who require your expertise to address the challenges they face. Clients are out there, but they won't be found—and they almost certainly won't find you—unless you're putting in the time, and taking the actions, necessary to become more visible and build strong relationships. The reason most private-practice lawyers fail to build robust practices is that they don't invest enough of themselves in what should be their top priority: developing new business.

This problem is not new or novel. Lawyers, as they always have, feel stretched thin and receive little training and guidance on how to build a practice. They tend to focus much more on the *practice* of law than the *business* of law. They learn, often when it's too late, that the business of law—in particular, business development—should have been a much higher priority throughout their careers.

Selling legal services is a uniquely challenging endeavor. Despite all the talk of innovation, the legal industry remains the same as it ever was, in that its product—the time and attention of lawyers—is expected to sell itself. Lawyers sell expertise and then apply it. Unlike in other multibillion dollar industries, with the exception of some adjacent professional services, such as management consulting, there is no separate sales function in law firms. There is no team tasked solely with the responsibility to sell. Lawyers must solve difficult problems on behalf of clients, which requires time and specialized expertise. They also must sell, which also takes time and a wholly different skill set. And, as has always been the case, lawyers struggle to balance their dual responsibilities, and many burn out in the process of trying. I experienced this struggle firsthand.

I went to law school in hopes of finding a respectable job that provided a steady paycheck. I graduated from a top law school in 2001 and started working at a well-regarded international law firm. I worked hard, earned a good living, and became competent at the practice of law. Mission accomplished... or so it seemed.

It was only after leaving the employ of a law firm and starting my own that I learned what it takes to excel at the business of law. Before striking out on my own—during the days when my paycheck dutifully arrived twice a month—I could focus only on serving my clients. However, they weren't actually *my clients*. I, like most of my colleagues, was merely doing the work, while a small number of lawyers within the firm were out developing the business.

Everything changed nearly a decade later. At that point, I was living in Detroit, and in May, 2009, I started a small law firm along with a partner who also took the leap from "BigLaw" to "SmallLaw." We jumped at the height of the financial crisis, on the cusp of the automotive industry meltdown, and just a couple of years before the City of Detroit's own bankruptcy filing. At least on paper, it wasn't the ideal time to start an entrepreneurial venture.

Looking back, it was, in fact, the perfect time. Fear and adversity can be great forms of motivation.

You may have already guessed the punchline here, which is that we built a successful law firm because of, not in spite of, the adversity we faced. The fear of not making a paycheck due to the difficult economic environment—heck, even being able to make payroll for our employees or pay for our office lease—is what drove us to be out hunting for business. We gave speeches, took clients to lunch, wrote articles, tapped referral sources, and attended conferences. We hustled in ways we never had in the comfortable confines of an established law firm.

I learned a great deal during those years. The most important lesson was gaining an understanding of the type of sustained and focused effort that is required to build a legal practice. Before starting my own firm, I focused exclusively on racking up billable hours. I worked so hard during my years at big firms that it often seemed like there was little room for anything else in my life. I barely had time for friends and family, let alone business development. At least that's how it felt at the time. It was only after facing the prospect of financial insecurity as a small law firm founder, far removed from the trappings, resources, and safety net of big firm life, that I learned how to bill plenty of hours, devote sufficient time to building a practice, and achieve greater work-life balance.

I feel fortunate for having had that experience. I'm not sure I would have ever learned what it takes to develop business otherwise.

I wrote this book because I know most lawyers have a desire to build a practice, but since the environments in which they work don't necessarily make their livelihoods dependent on it (at least for significant portions of their careers), they must rely on internal fortitude, not solely external pressures, to do it.

The period from 2010 to the beginning of 2020 was a pretty good time to be a lawyer. At most firms, over the course of the last decade, there was plenty of work to go around. And there's the rub. In that type of environment, it's possible to comfortably coast along in service of your colleagues who have clients. However, as we know from ancient Greek philosopher Heraclitus, "The only constant in life is change."

As we're learning from the effects of the COVID-19 crisis, external pressures always rear up to disrupt the good times. It happened in 2001, 2008, and it's happening again. The only thing unpredictable about these pressures is their origin, not their eventuality. Their predictably unpredictable nature should make us better at planning for them, but as discussed in the chapters to come, our biases toward short-term rewards inhibit our abilities to prepare for the long term. As a result, from big law firms to individual lawyers, external pressures expose our weaknesses more swiftly and significantly than we could have imagined. They deepen and accelerate trends we fail to adapt to because we think we have more time to adjust than we, in fact, do.

Even when times are good, pressures arise that many are unprepared for. Every year, at law firms across the country, when associates are being evaluated for partnership, and partners are being evaluated for profit-sharing, lawyers get caught flat-footed. As the day of reckoning approaches, lawyers realize that they should have been more focused on business development, but it's too late to do anything about it, because building a practice takes years to accomplish.

Lawyers typically don't avoid business development because they don't know what to do. There is a massive amount of information available about what it takes to build a practice. And there's no one-size-fits-all formula that works. Different lawyers use different approaches for business development, and there's no shortage of books, articles, podcasts, and other resources available to learn more about them.

No, business development procrastination doesn't result from ignorance—unless it's willful ignorance. It occurs because we perceive business development as something that is uncomfortable, perhaps awkward, and definitely risky from an emotional standpoint, because there is always a risk of failure or rejection. To one degree or another, we know what must be done. However, just as we know we should be going to the gym and eating more vegetables, but don't, we avoid it.

Since transitioning out of my law firm almost a decade ago, I've been coaching and training lawyers on the best practices involved in building a practice. My clients have used many different tactics to develop business. Some are aggressive networkers who are always out meeting new people and nurturing relationships. Others are prolific writers who create and publish thought-leadership content in the marketplace of ideas. All have one thing in common: They have systems and processes in place that enable them to devote the time necessary to develop new business, while at the same time serving their clients. They don't necessarily work harder than other lawyers who spend almost all of their time doing billable work for clients; they've just learned to work smarter.

Despite how busy you are, how difficult it may seem,

and how many times you've tried and failed before, you can excel at both the practice of law *and* the business of law. And in this moment, as we adjust to a world and an industry still coming to grips with the effects of the COVID-19 crisis, you can't afford not to prioritize the time and effort necessary to build a practice.

In this book, we will go step-by-step through the process that successful lawyers use to motivate themselves and manage their attention so they have the time—and the mental and emotional strength—necessary to develop business. We will cover best practices that are rooted in academic research and you will learn from the experiences of top performers across multiple domains.

This book is not merely a collection of disparate and unrelated productivity tips or hacks. Rather, it lays out a comprehensive system that will: (1) challenge you to determine what you really desire out of your life and career, (2) prompt you to examine your limiting beliefs about what you're capable of accomplishing, and (3) provide you with some fresh and unconventional ideas that will transform the way you think about productivity. I purposefully avoided laying out dozens of productivity tips because massive amounts of information won't solve the problem. Information is plentiful—there are plenty of books out there that spray the productivity-tips firehose. What is required is a fundamental mindset change.

You must pivot from your belief that business development is something you merely fit in when you can find the time, and instead start treating it as your most important priority.

Throughout the book I use the term "productivity" because it's helpful shorthand, but before we dive in, I think it's worth defining what I mean by it. To start, productivity *doesn't mean* merely going faster and faster. As most of us who have practiced law have experienced, that's a recipe for burnout and ineffectiveness. I consider productive lawyers to be ones who identify and focus on the small number of actions that drive the majority of their results. In other words, productive lawyers succeed because they distinguish between what is important and what is not, and create systems that allow them to work in accordance with their most important priorities.

Your goal should not be merely to be busy. Your goal should be to become as *effective* as possible. A busy lawyer is not necessarily an effective one. However, an effective lawyer is almost always busy, too. However, their busyness is directed toward high-priority, high-leverage tasks, leading to far better results. As we will discuss, those results include monetary rewards and advancement within a law firm, and also—and most important—a greater sense of autonomy in one's life and legal career.

As a preview, here are some of the foundational principles that we will address in the chapters to come:

Vision: Success starts with getting clear on what you want way out in the future so you can know what steps are required, starting today, to get you there.

Goals: A big vision for the future must be reduced to an achievable goal. A goal should not merely be an intention, but rather a commitment to uncompromisingly pursue your most desired professional outcome. A clear goal allows you to affirm your vision and establish systems that guide your day-to-day actions.

Goal Deconstruction: Making progress on long-term objectives is all about deconstructing your goals into specific action steps within the constraints of allotted time. We will discuss the importance of working backward to understand the component parts of your long-term goal, establishing a series of smaller goals based on that understanding, and then creating a plan that will keep you on track. You should deconstruct your big goal to the point where you have a clear understanding of the appropriate action you should be taking today—at this very moment—to be on the right path.

Time: In chapter 4, I challenge you to do something you may now believe is impossible, or at best improbable, which is to devote one hour of time each workday to business development activities. The reason lawyers resist the idea of spending what is, for most, merely ten percent of their time each day focused on business development, is that they view the pursuit of billable hours in the service of clients as their highest calling; the key to their long-term success. But that is short-term thinking. Instead of selling all of your time to clients to help them achieve their objectives, we will discuss the imperative of *selling yourself* one hour of your time every day to achieve your own.

Focus: Meaningful productivity results from understanding what you *should* do, not merely what you *can* do, to advance toward realizing your vision of building a profitable practice and having more autonomy at work.

Leverage: Yes, you probably can do most things on your to-do list better and faster than anyone else. No, you shouldn't try to do everything all by yourself. Better yet, have you stopped to consider whether many of the things you do even need to be done in the first place? Lawyers who generate significant results for their clients *and themselves* leverage their time by working only on their most important priorities, and delegate or eliminate everything else.

Building a productivity habit that will enable you to build a practice isn't easy. It probably won't happen quickly. It is possible, however.

Many have done it in the past, and are doing it now, which means you can, too. The fact that you're reading this book suggests that, even If you haven't yet built a practice, you're motivated enough by the prospect of doing so that you're taking an important first step forward, which is arming yourself with the understanding of what is necessary to succeed. Are you ready? There is no time like right now to find out what you're capable of.

PART 1:

THE
BIG
PICTURE

Cast a Clear Vision

"If you are working on something exciting
that you really care about, you don't have
to be pushed. The vision pulls you."

– STEVE JOBS

B ronnie Ware is a palliative nurse in Australia. She spent years counseling and caring for patients on their deathbeds. During the course of her work, she began to record the regrets of those at the end of their lives, and chronicled them in a book called *The Top Five Regrets of the Dying.* The most common regret was this:

"I wish I'd had the courage to live a life true to myself, not the life others expected of me."

During more than ten years of practicing law, then another ten years coaching and consulting within the legal industry, I've had a unique opportunity to engage in discussions with hundreds of lawyers about their perceptions of where their careers are headed. Unfortunately, too many feel that they are on the wrong track. My anecdotal experience comports with the generally held belief in the legal industry that most lawyers are dissatisfied with their careers.

Surveys suggest that career dissatisfaction among lawyers, and even rates of depression, are on the rise. According to 2018 research conducted by the Hazelden Betty Ford Foundation and the American Bar Association Commission on Lawyer Assistance Programs, 21 percent of licensed, employed attorneys qualify as problem drinkers, 28 percent struggle with depression, and 19 percent exhibit symptoms of anxiety. The greatest incidence of these problems occurs in younger lawyers in the first ten years of practice.[1]

A number of factors are cited as purported root causes of the unhappiness epidemic in the profession, including overwork, stress, uninteresting work, and the adversarial nature of the law, to name a few. Undoubtedly, all those are contributing factors. Less clear, at least on the surface, is what the fix should be.

Money, which is often presumed to be the magic elixir, doesn't seem to be the answer. Data compiled by the American Bar Association shows that average lawyer pay has nearly doubled since 1997[2], yet at the same time we know that unhappiness, alcoholism, depression, and anxiety rates continue to pervade the profession. So what gives?

In my experience, at the core of most discontent is the lack of control lawyers perceive they have over their circumstances. The demands of the job are overwhelming. Clients expect 24/7 responsiveness. Lawyers who don't have their own books of business are also at the beck and call of their colleagues who do. An unwelcome email, phone call, or pleading from an adversary on a Friday afternoon can turn a weekend upside down.

In short, most lawyers lack *autonomy* over their time and circumstances. And research shows that "autonomy"—defined as "the feeling that your life—its activities and habits—are self-chosen and self-endorsed"—is the number one predictor of happiness for people across the general population.[3]

More important for our purposes is that autonomy is what brings lawyers the most well-being as well. That's a key finding of a study conducted by Florida State University College of Law professor Lawrence Krieger and University of Missouri (Columbia) psychology professor Kennon Sheldon. Their study found that while factors typically associated with success, such as money and status, "showed nil to small associations with lawyer well-being," autonomy is integral to career satisfaction.[4]

Conclusions about the connection between autonomy, job performance, and well-being harken back to the work of psychologist Edward Deci. In the 1970s, Deci conducted experiments in which he attempted to incentivize one group of students to solve puzzles by offering them money, and compared their performance to another group of students who received no incentive. Deci found that those who were offered money were less interested in solving puzzles than those who weren't; the second group worked on the puzzles for a longer period of time and with more interest.

In a follow-up study of workers at an investment bank, Deci and his colleague Richard Ryan found that managers who offered "autonomy support"—which involved providing substantive feedback, greater freedom over how to tackle job duties, and encouragement—resulted in employees having more satisfaction and better performance.

Autonomy is an essential component of a concept in psychology called self-determination theory. Deci and Ryan introduced the idea of self-determination theory in their 1985 book, *Self-Determination and Intrinsic Motivation in Human Behavior*, in which they argued that people gain and sustain motivation through a desire to continually grow and improve.

Not just any form of motivation, however, is sufficient for high performance. Deci and Ryan concluded that forms of "extrinsic motivation," such as money and status, tend not to work very well. On the other hand, internal sources of motivation—"intrinsic motivation"— such as a desire to gain competence and independence, are what fuel growth. When people feel in control of their circumstances—in other words, feel autonomous—they tend to feel self-determined and perform at a high level.

While external motivation is not irrelevant—compensation is undeniably important—it's not enough to sustain someone over the course of a challenging career such as the practice of law. That's why it's important to feel more self-determined about your circumstances, and draw energy from intrinsic motivation by connecting your productivity to a higher purpose. Productivity is a means to an end, not an end in itself. If you're hoping to have a successful, fulfilling, and happy career, then, as the research suggests, it's critical to gear your productivity toward gaining greater autonomy. We'll discuss what that means and requires, in practical terms, shortly.

ARE YOU GAINING OR LOSING AUTONOMY?

If you're reading this book, then you probably have the desire, but perhaps feel like you lack the power, to make meaningful decisions in order to guide the direction of your career. When you lack autonomy, it's like being caught in the flow of a river, drifting wherever the current takes you. It feels like you're trying to steer a rudderless ship. Each day is dictated by other people's priorities, not your own. If you spend enough time drifting, it's easy to forget where you were headed in the first place—if you ever knew.

Too many lawyers suffer through these circumstances. The stress and overwhelm of the job consumes them. They're running on adrenaline, heading in the direction of where the next fire drill takes them. They work hard in search of milestones such as making partner and achieving a well-heeled retirement, but they're not happy or satisfied while trying to get there—and often not even when they do get there.

They're lost because they lost their autonomy along the way. All of the hard work and sacrifice served a purpose, but not their own. The relentless pace and late nights came at the cost of their freedom.

But it doesn't have to be this way. You can take back control. And even if you're feeling discouraged, you can decide today to stop allowing your fate in the legal profession to be dictated by the whims of others. As you move through this book, you'll learn about a number of specific actions you can take to wrest back control of your future. Before diving into specific action steps, however, let's pause and consider a few questions.

What do you desire? What are your career objectives? Where do you see yourself in 5, 10, or 25 years? These types of questions are important, because the path to autonomy begins with getting clear on what you truly want.

If you find yourself stuck in neutral, it's probably because you don't have a clear target in mind for your future. If you spend your days doing uninspiring work for clients (internal and external) who you'd rather not work with, it's likely the result of not having a defined, specific vision for your future. If you never draw a line in the sand and clarify what is really important to you, then you'll end up doing what's expected of you. If you're not sure what you really want, you'll spend your time doing the bidding of others.

Why would you expect to be satisfied with what you're doing on a day-to-day basis if you've never taken the time to get clear on what you really want out of your career?

Only you can know what it means to live a life true to yourself—one marked by self-directed, autonomous decisions and actions. Only you will know, as you get older, whether you attacked your life and career with passion and zest, and chased your dreams with vigor and enthusiasm. Regret comes from the choices we make, or don't make, at every step and stage of our lives. As lawyers, we spend so much of our time at work, the decisions we make during the course of our careers have a major impact on whether we look back on our lives with either a sense of fulfillment or feelings of regret.

The odds are that you'll spend more waking time at the office working than you will engaged in any other activity during the course of your life. This should be sobering, but need not be a source of despair. The practice of law can be a great and noble profession. As a lawyer, you have the opportunity to make a real difference in other people's lives— something few people can say about their work—and also be intellectually engaged and become financially secure. But career satisfaction and success won't happen by accident. It all starts with getting clear on what you want way out in the future so you can know what steps are required, starting today, to get you there.

THE POWER OF
LONG-TERM THINKING

If I was to offer you $100 today or $120 a week from now, which would you choose? While thought experiments aren't the same as real-world experiences, if you're like most people you'd choose the hundred bucks now. That's the conclusion of a classic study which found that, when it comes to making decisions, most of us opt for immediate gratification.[5]

Why does this matter? Well, succeeding in a law firm is all about balancing your desire for short-term versus long-term rewards, and prioritizing your time and attention in congruence with your personal objectives.

For example, an associate who has no intention or desire to make partner at a law firm would likely optimize for the billable hour, because the economic incentives in most law firms would provide them with greater short-term financial rewards for doing so.

A long-term thinking associate who hopes to make partner, however, would balance billable time with a greater emphasis on non-billable time. They would understand that the old apprenticeship law firm model, in which associates were (and, in some cases, still are) encouraged to "keep your head down and do good work" has changed. They would appreciate that associates who are elected into a partnership are those who have unique skill sets and demonstrable business development acumen. These qualities—unique skill sets and business development acumen—take considerable amounts of time and effort to develop, so if partnership and its long-term rewards are the objective, the rational thing to do would be to invest in them throughout one's career as an associate.

The same is true of a partner hoping to build a book of

business. One of the most effective ways to generate business is to become known as a narrowly focused expert within a particular industry. It's not that being a well-rounded lawyer is a bad thing. A lawyer with depth and breadth of knowledge is obviously a valuable asset to a client. The problem is that positioning oneself as providing "full service" or possessing "general knowledge" is often ineffective from a brand-positioning standpoint. Lawyers who cast really wide nets believe that chasing the biggest market possible offers them a better opportunity to acquire a greater number of clients. But most quickly learn that the exact opposite is true. You can't be all things to all people and expect to make an impact. Clients are seeking out specialized experts to solve specific problems.

Building a niche-focused practice, however, is a long-term proposition. The rewards that await at the end of the process are significant, but it can take a long time—often years—of concerted, focused effort to get to the point where you're generating the inbound opportunities and high hourly rates that narrowly focused lawyers command. During the process of trying to build a niche practice, many lawyers get off track because they can't resist taking on matters that fall outside of their areas of focus. These short-term diversions distract them from what they're trying to build. One case leads to another, and before long they're taking on whatever comes in the door. As a result, they never develop the expert reputations they set out to build, and they end up in an endless cycle of chasing commodity work throughout their careers.

The point is, we're all affected by cognitive biases that lead to suboptimal decision-making. While we all prefer big rewards over smaller ones, most of us have an even stronger preference for present rewards over future ones—even when the future ones are much more valuable. This phenomenon, a type of cognitive bias, is called "hyperbolic discounting." It stands for the proposition that the further away a reward is in the future, the less of an immediate motivation there is to put the work in to realize it. Therefore, the tendency to value short-term rewards is a drag on one's ability to achieve long-term success. The types of actions that are going to make you look good in the short term, such as optimizing for billable hours over engaging in business development, are what will hamper you over the long term.

When you have a clear vision for the future, however, it's far easier to resist the allure of short-term thinking, and to accept the trade-offs that are required along the way to realize your vision.

THERE'S NO SUCH THING AS AN "OVERNIGHT SUCCESS"

In almost every professional endeavor, and across every industry, it takes years of practice, persistence, and patience to gain mastery and make a big impact. The idea of achieving "overnight success" is a myth, and it's one perpetuated by those who peddle short-term solutions. History is replete with success stories of people who seemingly burst onto the scene, but in reality toiled for years in anonymity in pursuit of their long-term visions.

The first time that almost anyone outside of small circles within the technology and entertainment industries became aware of Pixar Animation Studios president Ed Catmull was following the release of *Toy Story* in 1995. But Catmull's dream to make the first fully computer-generated animated feature film began decades before. He conceived of the idea as a young computer scientist in the early 1970s, well before the technology existed to make it possible. After finishing graduate school, Catmull estimated it would take ten years to achieve his dream. It ended up taking more than 20.

One of the most interesting aspects of Catmull's story is that, following graduation, he turned down a job offer from Disney. On the surface, Disney seemed to offer the clearest and safest path available to someone whose goal was to make animated movies. Catmull had dreamed of working at Disney ever since he was a young boy. However, Catmull perceived Disney's filmmaking prowess and creativity to be on the decline, so he passed. Instead, he took a job with the New York Institute of Technology as the director of the organization's new computer graphics lab. He was then hired by *Star Wars* creator George Lucas to run a new animation and computer graphics initiative at LucasFilms.

In 1986, Lucas, no longer able to subsidize Catmull's animation work, sold the division to Steve Jobs for $10 million. Pixar was born, but *Toy Story* wouldn't be released for almost ten more years. The technology and financing required to make a digitally animated feature film weren't yet available. In the interim, Catmull and his team began manufacturing and selling the computer graphics technology they had developed to other businesses. Pixar needed to survive and Jobs demanded a return on his investment.

Catmull scraped, clawed, and cajoled his team along, never losing sight of his ultimate objective. Finally, in the early 1990s, he and Jobs struck a deal with Disney to finance and distribute what would become *Toy Story*. Catmull's story has a Hollywood ending. In 2006, Disney bought Pixar for $7.4 billion.

To the outside world, Catmull and Pixar catapulted to success. But their journey was long and arduous. Jobs was later quoted as saying, "Pixar is seen by a lot of folks as an overnight success, but if you really look closely, most overnight successes took a long time."

The most successful author in history has a similar story. J.K. Rowling had a difficult childhood. Rowling's mother was diagnosed with multiple sclerosis when Rowling was 15 years old. She died a decade later. After college, Rowling worked at the research desk for Amnesty International, performing translation work. At 26, she moved to Portugal, taught English, got married, and had a child.

Following Rowling's separation from her husband, she moved back to England and lived off government welfare. After years of fits and starts she began working in earnest on her first novel, a fanciful story of a young wizard named Harry Potter. She sent her manuscript to numerous publishers, all of whom, if they responded at all, rejected her work. Ultimately, she sold the book to a small publisher in England and received an advance of a few thousand pounds.

The rest, of course, is history. But what's noteworthy about Rowling's story is that she never wavered in her belief that she would become a successful author. As she said in her 2008 Harvard University commencement speech, "I was convinced that the only thing I wanted to do, ever, was to write novels."

It's important to have a big, bold, ambitious vision for the future. But make no mistake; there are no shortcuts on the journey. In this sense, success is like an iceberg. Only a small tip of an iceberg is visible above water, but a mass of ice lies hidden below the surface. The same is true of success. We see the outcome but not always the hard work and dedication required to achieve it.

OPTIMIZE FOR AUTONOMY

So what does all this talk of dreams, desires, and struggles have to do with productivity? After all, isn't productivity all about implementing tips, tricks, and hacks that allow you to squeeze more work in during your day?

While that may be the conventional understanding of productivity's purpose, it's not one that's going to make you a better, more satisfied lawyer. Working faster is not the answer. If you're a busy lawyer, you're undoubtedly moving fast, but is your movement purposeful and are you headed in the right direction?

"Each day in the office is like another day on the hamster wheel," one of my coaching clients, Josh, told me. As a busy litigator with hefty billable hour requirements, he was always concerned that he wouldn't have enough work on his plate, despite often being faced with way more work than he could handle. Every morning, the moment he sat down at his desk, he would start processing the emails that had poured in overnight, and by the time he got through them, a new batch would have arrived. Meetings, phone calls, depositions, drafting briefs, court appearances—and more emails—dominated his days. Each day resembled the next. "As soon as I get through one task, I am on to the next. There is never any time to work on anything other than client work," he told me.

Josh's story is not unique. He sought out coaching because he reached a point where he couldn't handle his crushing workload. What he thought he needed was advice on how to become more productive. But what he really required was focus.

In particular, he needed to bring into clear focus what he really wanted out of his career, not just today, but, more importantly, in the future. He had been operating in default mode—driven solely by the relentless urgency of day-to-day circumstances—and as a result he had completely lost sight of any long-term career objectives.

He came to realize that simply moving faster to get more billable work done during the day was not the answer. He understood that would result in nothing more than maintaining the status quo. The faster he moved, the more client work there was. That prospect was untenable to him, so he took it upon himself to stop and consider what he really wanted, and changed the course of his career and life in the process.

The steps Josh had to take to transform were not easy. But with a clear vision in mind, he had a target at which to aim and path to follow. No longer were his days dictated by others. For the first time in his career, he felt like he was in control.

Like Josh, who finally got serious about changing his circumstances for the better, it's time for you to get to work. The first challenge I pose to you in this book is simple but not easy. Stop. Step away from your desk. Find an environment in which you can think clearly.

If you're going to tackle the important work of casting a vision for your future, you need to clear your head and limit distractions. This is not the type of work that can be done amid the chaos of a law firm office. Leaders who craft a clear vision for themselves and others invest the time necessary to focus on the long term in an environment that fosters clear, creative thinking.

When he was the CEO of Microsoft, Bill Gates would disconnect twice a year for off-site "Think Weeks" during which he would do nothing but read and think deeply. His family, friends, and Microsoft employees were not invited. He read papers from Microsoft associates on topics related to the future of technology and emerging product trends. Gates typically read 100 or more papers during a Think Week. These sessions led to many Microsoft innovations and new initiatives.

I'm not suggesting that you, as a busy lawyer, are in a position to go off on a two-week monastic retreat to ponder your future. What I am saying is that you, like Gates, need to stop for more than a mere moment to create the time and space necessary to think clearly and strategically about where your career is currently headed and where you want it to go.

I know asking you to "stop" may seem antithetical to most of the productivity advice you've heard or read which pushes you to "go" faster and faster. But the consequences of aiming your productivity toward the wrong long-term vision are too grave to not invest the time necessary to get it right.

If you're a lawyer working in a law firm and you're dissatisfied with your current circumstances, the result of this introspection may be a decision to pursue an alternative path. You can try your hand at an in-house position. You can walk away altogether to tackle a career outside the law. And if the path you choose is an alternative one, there are important principles you'll learn in this book that will help you no matter where your career takes you.

This book, however, is geared specifically to those of you who are committed to building a successful and satisfying career within a law firm. And if that's your long-term vision, the best way to achieve it is to aim for greater autonomy. As we've already discussed, autonomy—not money, power, or status—is the number one predictor of happiness and satisfaction in a person's life and career. Accordingly, you'd be wise to optimize for it.

That's easier said than done, however. So how does one gain autonomy in a law firm?

As Krieger and Sheldon address in their study on lawyer happiness, law firms should play an important role in fostering autonomy through thoughtful policy-making, mentoring, and training. While employers surely can do more, don't count on anyone, or any firm, to bestow you with greater autonomy. That sort of expectation is antithetical to the entire notion of being an autonomous individual who exhibits independence, is self-reliant, and draws upon intrinsic motivation. If you want to gain greater control, it's on you to make it happen.

GAIN MORE AUTONOMY BY BUILDING A BOOK OF BUSINESS

Whether you're a fourth-year associate or a freshly minted partner, the key to a more autonomous future while working at a law firm lies in building your own practice. Depending on what stage you're at in your career, what size firm you work at, and your ambition, the work required to acquire clients will be different.

If you're at a relatively early stage in your career, you should be laying a foundation for future business development by focusing on expanding your network, honing your expertise in your area of practice, and publishing thought-leadership content. If you're at a later stage where there is a greater expectation—your own and that of your firm—that you should be generating business now, then you'll need to be engaged in more active, urgent prospecting. We'll get into more detail about how to create a productivity system that enables you to engage in robust business development efforts in the chapters to come. For now, simply open yourself up to the idea that building a book of business is the path to a brighter future.

Having clients is important for many reasons. A loyal stable of clients is the most valuable form of career currency that a lawyer can have. A lawyer with clients is not only a valued asset in their own firm, they are attractive to others as well. Clients create leverage for lawyers because there's value in having others working on your matters. You'll be freed up to devote more time to develop more business, and you'll get a piece of the revenue others generate when they do work for your clients. At most firms, having a book of business (or at least demonstrating a strong ability to develop one) is a prerequisite to making partner. It increases one's compensation. Most importantly, it's empowering. Having clients allows lawyers to have greater autonomy over their careers and personal lives because they're not reliant upon others for work.

This book is meant to present a realistic—not a romanticized—view of the practice of law. Accordingly, it's important to acknowledge that having a roster of your own clients is not easy. It creates a whole new set of pressures and responsibilities. When you own the client relationship, you own the ultimate responsibility to produce great work and provide great client service in order to maintain the relationship. When something goes wrong, you also own the responsibility to fix it.

But in a choice between the alternatives of having or not

having a book of business, having clients gives you far more options. Lawyers who desire more autonomy will likely never get it if they're dependent on others for billable hours. With clients, a lawyer will make more money, have more options, and be in a position to exercise more control—in other words, have more autonomy.

This begs an obvious question: If building a profitable book of business is so important, then why don't more lawyers, young and old, prioritize it, let alone accomplish it? The problem is not one of knowledge. Most of us *know* what we need to be doing. It's not one of desire. Lawyers *want* the benefits that come with building a book of business. The problem is one of action—or, in this case, lack of it. We equivocate and procrastinate, despite knowing how important it is for us to act.

That's where productivity comes in. It's only through consistent, concerted action that you will put yourself in a position to reap the rewards from building a book of business. Always keep in mind, however, that merely becoming more productive isn't the end you should be striving for. Productivity should be seen as a means to whatever end you desire. That's why it's critical to craft a long-term vision that keeps you intrinsically motivated. If you're fixated on external motivators—like money and status—that have little correlation with long-term career satisfaction, then you'll be left to rely on willpower alone in your push to become more productive. If your vision—your end—is to become more autonomous, you'll be intrinsically motivated to do the work necessary to build a better life and career for yourself. To succeed, link your productivity to a higher purpose, which is reflected in your long-term vision.

Chapter Summary

The pace of the practice of law provides few opportunities for lawyers to stop and think strategically about the future. As a result, too many lawyers drift aimlessly from one year to the next, rather than marching forward with confidence that they're headed toward a destination of their own design.

To get clear on your long-term objectives, you must set aside the time to think and reflect. This can't be done in the midst of the whirlwind of your daily routine. You must invest the time necessary to cast a vision for the future, because your productivity must be aligned with a higher, more significant purpose than a desire to bill more hours.

When you neglect the work necessary to establish a clear vision for the future, you default to being motivated by extrinsic forms of motivation, such as money and status. But research suggests—and our own intuitions and experiences tell us—that such forms of motivation aren't all that motivating. Instead, it's important to optimize for autonomy. When you feel in control of your circumstances at work, you'll feel more satisfied about your work. And the best way to gain autonomy in a law firm is to build a practice.

COACHING NOTE:
Write Down Your Long-Term
Vision Statement

Casting a vision for your future requires clear thinking and an investment of time. You need to be able to envision and articulate your ideal future before you can start working toward it. Use the Vision Statement template at **www.productivitypivot.com** to help you think through the critical issues. Begin by defining what your ideal life and career looks like five years down the road, then describe what you stand to gain—what it will feel like, what you will have achieved—when you realize your vision.

2

Set Ambitious Goals

"If you want to be happy, set a goal that commands your thoughts, liberates your energy and inspires your hopes."

– ANDREW CARNEGIE

olin O'Brady set out in search of adventure after graduating from Yale in 2006. Before settling into the world of cubicles and conference rooms, he wanted to experience new countries and cultures. At 22 years of age, he was smart and athletic, with a degree in economics and NCAA Division 1 swimming experience under his belt.[6]

A post-graduation backpacking trip around the world led

him to Thailand, and a moonlit beach party on the island of Ko Tao. As is common on many Thai beaches, revelers were engaging in different forms of fire dancing, including hopping over large, flaming jump ropes.

O'Brady decided to partake, and what happened next changed the course of his life in ways he could not have imagined. It was one of those experiences that you would never wish for, but never change because of its transformative impact.

He stepped up to the jump rope with shorts on and no shoes, prepared to leap, and then things went horribly wrong. Instead of clearing the rope, it wrapped around his legs. His body instantly caught fire.

Fortunately, he was near the ocean and ran straight toward it to douse the flames that had engulfed him up to his neck. He suffered serious burns over 25 percent of his body. His feet and legs were badly burned.

He was rushed on a moped down a dirt road to the nearest medical facility, a rural one-room nursing station. He endured eight surgeries over the course of the next week. There was a cat running around his bed in the ramshackle "hospital" each day when he emerged from surgery. His doctors told him that he likely would never walk normally again due to extensive scar tissue damage.

O'Brady spent five days alone in unbearable circumstances suffering from excruciating pain before his mom could reach his bedside. She remained with him in Thailand for months, and helped nurse him back to health—physically, emotionally, and psychologically.

She knew that for her son to recover he must, despite his current hardship, look forward with hope and optimism about the future. She wanted him to envision life beyond the obstacles of the moment. She challenged him to set a goal.

Notwithstanding how absurd it seemed given his condition, he established an ambitious goal to compete in a triathlon.

After months of recovery in Thailand, O'Brady returned to the United States, moved to Chicago, and took a job as a commodities broker. He endured grueling physical rehabilitation, learned to walk again, and began to take steps (literal and figurative) to honor the promise he had made to his mom—and himself—from his hospital bed in Thailand. He started training for the swim, bike, and run disciplines involved in triathlon racing.

O'Brady signed up for the 2009 Chicago Triathlon, which was to take place approximately 18 months after he suffered his injuries. The Chicago Triathlon is an Olympic-distance race, which means he would need to swim 1,500 meters, bike 40 kilometers, and run 10 kilometers.

Not only did O'Brady finish the race, he won it, which triggered a remarkable string of events so far-fetched they may not have made it into a fictional Hollywood screenplay.

After his Chicago victory, O'Brady quit his commodities trading job and began training and competing as a professional triathlete. In 2016, after retiring from triathlon competition, O'Brady set out to conquer the "Explorers Grand Slam," which involves climbing the highest mountain on each of the seven continents and reaching both the North and South Poles. In May 2016, O'Brady reached the summit of Denali in Alaska, completing the Explorers Grand Slam in 137 days. He crushed the world record for completing the feat by 60 days.

He then set the world record for the "Three Poles Challenge," becoming the fastest person to reach the South Pole, North Pole, and the summit of Mount Everest. He followed that accomplishment by setting another world record for the "50 US High Points Challenge," reaching the highest point in each of the 50 states in just 21 days, 9 hours, and 48 minutes.

O'Brady then took things up another notch. In December 2018, he became the first person to ever complete a solo and unassisted trek across Antarctica. For 54 days, over 932 miles, he pulled a sled carrying hundreds of pounds of food and supplies across the most frigid and unforgiving terrain on the planet.

O'Brady is a freak of nature. His accomplishments seem superhuman, and therefore his experience is mostly unrelatable. But this is inescapable: He's human, and therefore subject to the same self-doubts and limiting beliefs that we all grapple with and that stand in the way of our progress. And yet he wills himself to do remarkable things despite the challenges—such as regaining the ability to walk, then run and climb—that stand in his way.

You can, too. Indeed, you can do more than you imagine is possible when you set your mind to a desired result, particularly when you, like O'Brady, crystallize your intentions into clear, specific, and actionable goals. Casting a clear vision for your future is an important first step, but good intentions are never enough. *You must define with specificity what you will achieve through goal-setting.*

Would O'Brady have retrained his ability to walk after his accident if his mom had not pushed him to set the goal of racing in a triathlon? Probably. But would he have gone on to set numerous world records while completing some of the toughest physical challenges imaginable? Almost certainly not. Setting a difficult goal, and then achieving it, allowed him to gain the confidence and create the momentum necessary to imagine what more might be possible. It set him on a path that would ultimately lead him—one step at a time—to the peak of Mount Everest, across Antarctica, and into the record books.

THE IMPORTANCE OF SETTING GOALS

When I coach attorneys in an effort to help them overcome the mental hurdles blocking them from building a book of business, I start by asking my clients a seemingly simple question: *What do you want?*

After an inevitable pause, I'll typically receive answers such as "I want more clients," "I want to make partner," or "I want to become more productive." The answers suggest my clients had some sort of vision in mind for the future—before the coaching process had even begun—yet they were stuck in neutral, unable to make progress.

When we want something, we all start with good intentions. But that's insufficient to create lasting change and positive results. When we fail to make progress, it's not because our intentions were flawed. It's because we never pivoted from intention to action.

Be honest with yourself. Is there anything you've undertaken in your life where you've utterly failed despite putting in your best effort? You may not have achieved the full extent of what you were hoping for, but I'd be willing to bet that even if you didn't get 100 percent of the way to your objective, there were still some positive takeaways from the experience.

Perhaps you studied like crazy for the LSAT in hopes of getting into a top-ten law school. Even if you didn't achieve your objective, you're probably doing just fine with your top-thirty law school degree, and have come to realize that the status of the school you attended diminishes in importance as you gain more experience practicing law. For those who didn't study but still had Ivy League ambitions? You can testify to how far good intentions will get you.

Desire must turn into *doing* if you want to make progress. First, however, you must determine what all that doing is going to be about. If you don't make a commitment to yourself to shift from vision to action, then you'll likely stay put in your circumstances. Without a clear end point in mind, you'll bounce from one idea to another, constantly in motion but not moving in any particular direction.

As we make the transition from casting a vision to setting a goal, let's take a moment to define the words "vision" and "goal," because many people mistakenly use them interchangeably. They're not the same thing. A vision (for example, building a book of business that gives you greater autonomy) is the destination you want to reach. The destination may be clear but the path to get there isn't. Goals allow you to determine the path you must travel to realize your vision, and they serve as milestones along the way. A vision is the end. Goals are the means.

To reinforce the distinction between vision and goals, and highlight its importance, let's examine the approach of the man who is arguably the most successful entrepreneur of our time, if not all time, Jeff Bezos, CEO of Amazon and founder of aerospace company Blue Origin.

Bezos has cast bold visions for both companies. In 1995, while operating Amazon out of his garage, Bezos crafted an ambitious vision statement for Amazon in which he stated his intention to grow it into the "Earth's most customer-centric company."[7] In a speech at the Yale Club in New York City in 2019, Bezos explained that his mission for Blue Origin is to help create a way for the solar system to support 1 trillion people. That way, Bezos said, "we'd have 1,000 Mozarts, and 1,000 Einsteins."[8]

Now that's some bold thinking. However, while Bezos recognized in his speech that "vision is absolutely important," he explained that it wasn't enough. To realize his vision for his companies, Bezos said, "we've got to get started." Getting started requires setting clear goals that, once achieved, will move you closer to realizing your vision.

In the case of Amazon, its efforts to offer a huge inventory of products at the lowest prices possible, one- or two-day delivery of products, the Kindle, its foray into groceries through its acquisition of Whole Foods, and a broad array of other initiatives, all resulted from goals Amazon set with its vision of becoming the "Earth's most customer-centric company" in mind.

"You need a vision, then, that's a touchstone. It's something you can always come back to if you ever get confused," Bezos said. "But mostly, your time should be spent on things that are happening today, this year, maybe in the next two to three years."

As Bezos has demonstrated through his visionary leadership, setting a goal that is ambitious, specific, and measurable allows you to both confirm your intentions *and* begin taking steps toward transformational change. Goal-setting is one of the most powerful tools you have at your disposal, no matter what you want to achieve in life. Virtually all coaches, corporate trainers, business leaders, and other experts use goal-setting as a key component of their processes to push others toward higher performance.

Despite how powerful goal-setting is, it's a massively underutilized tool by most individuals. In his book *Eat That Frog!: 21 Great Ways to Stop Procrastinating and Get More Done in Less Time*, human performance expert Brian Tracy wrote that only approximately three percent of adults have clear, written goals, yet those that do accomplish significantly more than those who have never taken the time to write out their goals.

Accordingly, goal-setting is not an exercise to overlook or take lightly. The stakes are too high to regard your professional goals the way you might a New Year's resolution, which most treat as negotiable and easily discarded without consequence. An effective goal is not merely an intention, but rather a commitment to uncompromisingly pursue your most desired professional outcome. A clear goal allows you to affirm your vision and establish a framework for your behavior. In each situation you confront, you're faced with a binary decision, the result of which will either take you closer toward what you want or further away from it. Without a clear goal in mind, your actions will be more likely to be driven by convenience rather than intention and purpose.

One of the most important reasons to set a goal, is that a goal serves as the precursor to a plan. On May 25, 1961, President John F. Kennedy announced a goal of putting a man on the Moon by the end of the decade. At the time of his speech, the United States lacked the technology and know-how necessary to carry out Kennedy's ambitious directive. But with the goal of putting a man on the Moon in mind, America's brightest minds got to work, and on July 20, 1969, they accomplished the mission. You can accomplish yours, too, if you set an ambitious goal and establish a plan to achieve it.

In the words of Pablo Picasso, "Our goals can only be reached through a vehicle of a plan, in which we must fervently believe, and upon which we must vigorously act. There is no other route to success."

While it's not always easy to settle upon a vision—after all, many of us struggle to determine what we want way out in the future—harder still is determining how we'll get from Point A (where we are) to Point B (where we want to go). Perhaps hardest of all is taking the first step forward. The secret to getting ahead? In almost all cases, it's simply getting started.

HOW TO SET EFFECTIVE GOALS

———

Don't worry if you've had trouble making progress on your goals in the past. That's an experience everyone can relate to. Consider this an opportunity to start anew.

With your Vision Statement in mind (if you haven't yet written down your Vision Statement, I encourage you to revisit the exercise described at the end of chapter 1), it's time to start thinking about reducing that vision into actionable goals. Goals help put the realization of your vision on a deadline.

The most well-known, and, in my experience as a business coach, the most effective technique for setting and achieving goals is the SMART goal framework, which is often attributed to the work of management consultant Peter Drucker. "SMART" stands for Specific, Measurable, Attainable, Realistic, and Time-bound.

One of the key benefits of using the SMART goal framework is that it forces you to clearly consider and define goals as you set them, thereby reducing the risk of creating vague, ambiguous goals that are unlikely to be achieved.

A SMART goal must be:

Specific: The more detailed and specific your goals are, the more likely you'll be to achieve them. Think about the last time you handed off an assignment to another attorney, a vendor, or your assistant. If your instructions were vague, did you get the results you were hoping for? Probably not, and the same principle applies to goal-setting. With SMART goals, you're providing instructions to yourself, so be specific. How specific should your goal be? "I will make more money this year" is too loose. "I will generate $500,000 in new business by December 31" makes it easier to visualize and achieve what you desire.

Measurable: To achieve your goals, you must measure your progress. Establishing clear parameters and identifying interim performance objectives is the only way to know whether you're on or off track. For example, "consistently meet with referral sources" is not measurable. What does "consistently" mean in this context? You need to have concrete metrics in place, such as "set up two meetings with referral sources every week," when establishing goals.

Attainable: It feels good to set lofty, ambitious goals— and you *should* aim to set a goal that pushes and stretches you to achieve higher performance. But if you aim too high, you may quickly get off track, become disheartened at your lack of progress, and give up altogether. That's a common occurrence when it comes to goal-setting. The objective isn't to radically transform overnight. It's to rack up small wins that build momentum and motivate you to push forward.

Realistic: You're a busy lawyer. Perhaps you have a big trial coming up this year. You may have a young child or an elderly relative to care for at home. In an ideal world, you'd have all the time in the world to make uninterrupted progress on your goals. But, of course, you live in the real world, not an ideal one, so make sure your goal-setting conforms with reality. You can do almost anything, just not all at once.

Time-Bound: Time flies when you're having fun, and also when you set out to achieve goals. If you're like most people, you may find yourself setting the same goals year after year because you made little to no progress in prior ones. Don't let yourself off the hook this time. Set an aggressive but realistic time frame for yourself to achieve your goals.

Put simply, when setting goals, you need to state specifically what you will do, by when, and have a means to verify whether you've achieved your objective. Anything less is too ephemeral.

There is one last tip on goal-setting that I want to share, and this one may be the most important of all. In fact, it may help double your odds of success. *Write down your goals.*

This advice may seem obvious, and you've probably heard it before, but it's so important that it bears repeating. Research shows the simple act of writing down your goals significantly increases your odds of achieving them. The act of reducing your goals to writing clarifies your intentions and forces you to get loosely held beliefs out of your head and into the world in the form of a clear written plan.

Gail Matthews, a psychology professor at Dominican University in California, did a study on goal-setting with 267 participants from a wide range of professions and countries. She found that people are 40 percent more likely to achieve their goals when they write them down.[9] In his best-selling book, *The Power of Habit: Why We Do What We Do in Life and Business*, Charles Duhigg discusses a study in which patients recovering from knee or hip surgery were given a booklet and instructed to write down their recovery goals and a detailed action plan to achieve them. Three months later, the patients who wrote down their goals were walking well before those who did not. They recovered almost twice as fast.

Goal-setting is akin to entering into a contract with yourself. So the next time you commit to achieving something, take the age-old advice you give your clients to heart: *Get it in writing.*

Chapter Summary

Having clear goals helps direct your focus toward actionable behaviors. With goals in mind, you'll act with more intention and purpose. If you set your goals to align with your long-term vision, and then act accordingly, you'll move forward with greater confidence and a higher degree of success.

The most effective way to establish and achieve important goals is by using the SMART goal framework. A SMART goal is Specific, Measurable, Attainable, Realistic, and Time-Bound. Because goal-setting is so critical to your success, you need to invest the time necessary to formulate—and then write down—your goals.

COACHING NOTE:
Write Down
Your SMART Goals

Establish and write down no more than three SMART goals for yourself using the SMART Goal Worksheet available at **www.productivitypivot.com.** Make sure your goals align with the Vision Statement you wrote down after reading chapter 1, and that you can realistically achieve your goals within a one-year timeframe.

3

Deconstruct Your Goals into an Actionable Plan

"A goal without a plan is just a wish."

– ANTOINE DE SAINT-EXUPÉRY

A s a kid, John dreamed of becoming a professional baseball player. When reality set in during his late teens, he decided to pursue a more practical path that may sound familiar. He earned an undergraduate accounting degree, then a law degree. Approaching the age of 30, John was busy with his legal career, working 60 to 70 hours a week at a law firm in a small town in Mississippi. He specialized in criminal defense and personal injury litigation.[10]

At court one day, John overheard the chilling testimony of a 12-year-old girl who had been raped. As a new dad, John became fixated on the story and began to wonder what would have happened if the girl's father had taken matters into his own hands and killed her rapists.

That moment of curiosity—the spark of an idea—set John on a path that would forever change his life, and ultimately transform an industry. He decided to write a novel inspired by the story he heard in the DeSoto County courthouse that day.

Like a childhood dream of becoming a professional baseball player, becoming a published author is another "pipe dream" that many people have. Polls suggest that approximately 80 percent of people want to write a book, but few ever do.[11] John, however, was committed.

He could not afford to stop practicing law to pursue what he perceived at the time as a writing hobby. He had a vision to become a successful author. His goal was to write and publish his first book. What he needed was a plan to make it happen in the midst of his hectic life.

To achieve his goal, John created a daily ritual for himself. He would wake up at 5 a.m. sharp, take a quick shower, and hustle to his office. He would be at his desk, coffee and legal pad in hand, by 5:30 a.m. As with most busy litigators, John would often have to be in court or in client meetings by no later than 9 a.m., so he knew those early hours would be critical for making progress.

His plan for achieving his goal was "SMART"—that is, specific, measurable, attainable, realistic, and time-bound: Write at least one page per day. Three years later, by sticking to his rigorous daily writing routine, John Grisham finished his first novel, *A Time to Kill*.

Years later, having sold over 300 million copies of his

books, Grisham still sets (and, without fail. achieves) a goal of writing one novel a year. One thing that's changed is that Grisham now has the luxury of starting his writing day at 7 a.m. rather than 5:30 a.m.—there are no more client deadlines or court appearances to worry about. What hasn't changed is Grisham's uncompromising dedication to making daily progress toward his goals.

When setting out to write his first novel, Grisham could have, like most people, fallen short of his goal by succumbing to the enormous task facing him. The idea of writing a novel is overwhelming. But writing one page—250 words—every day? That's the type of plan that's much more manageable.

That's not to say, however, that it's easy. As we covered in chapter 1, short-term desires often get in the way of the work required to accomplish long-term objectives. Grisham's desire for an hour more of sleep each morning could have easily derailed his progress. It would have been easy to skip a day of writing here or there to get in a bit more preparation for an upcoming trial. But Grisham didn't make a tepid commitment to write his first book. He set a clear goal and achieved it. And when it comes to achieving what you want out of your life and career, you should approach goal-setting with the same level of rigor. Once you commit 100 percent, you can't help but move forward with passion and purpose. If you're only 99 percent committed, you've created the wiggle room that puts the achievement of your goal in doubt.

When things get tough, and other urgent demands arise, it will be easy to opt out. There's always next year, you'll think. But then next year comes and the same pattern repeats. Every time you compromise your own priorities in service of someone else's, and as a result fall short of your goals, you make it harder to see yourself as someone who is capable of making positive change. Instead of the autonomy you seek, you become more beholden to the idea that your job is to help other people (your clients, your superiors) achieve their goals.

However, the only way you can effectively serve others is by making sure *your* priorities are met. There's a reason you're supposed to put on your own oxygen mask first before helping others with theirs on an airplane. If you want to succeed, you need to go all-in on yourself.

THINK BIG. ACT SMALL.

Even when they're otherwise committed, the thing that stops many lawyers from moving forward on a big, ambitious goal, such as developing a profitable roster of clients, is simply not knowing how to start. Their goals look great on paper but never translate into real-world action. They fixate on the results they want, can't possibly imagine fitting in all the work required to achieve them, and never get moving.

It's normal to feel resistance to getting started when setting out to accomplish something ambitious. But when resistance creeps in, remind yourself that it's not all the big, bold things we do during our lives and careers that lead to success. It's the small actions taken every day that make all the difference and lead to compounding results over time.

Author and marketing guru Seth Godin wrote on his blog: "The thing is, incremental daily progress (negative or positive) is what actually causes transformation. A figurative drip, drip, drip. Showing up, every single day, gaining in strength, organizing for the long haul, building connection, laying track—this subtle but difficult work is how culture changes."

It's how a lawyer's life and career changes, too.

One of the starkest examples of the power of small, incremental progress is what happened to the British cycling team in 2003 after hiring Dave Brailsford as its new performance director. At the time, the team was mired in mediocrity, to put it charitably. No British cyclist had ever won the Tour de France, and only one had won a gold medal in nearly 100 years at the Olympic Games.

Everything changed once Brailsford took over, but it didn't happen overnight. Brailsford instituted a series of small changes over the course of several years, each of which, in isolation, seemed insignificant. The changes included things like teaching riders how to properly wash their hands to reduce the risk of illness, bringing along pillows and linens while traveling to improve the sleep of riders in hotels, and making tweaks to jersey and seat designs.

All of those changes, and hundreds more like them, were part of the execution of Brailsford's strategy to harness what he called the "aggregation of marginal gains." And gain they did. Five years after Brailsford's arrival, the British team won 60 percent of the medals at the Olympic Games in Beijing. British riders then went on to win five Tour de France victories over the course of six years. Like consistent investments in the stock market over time, the British team's small improvements compounded into huge gains.

Just as writing 250 words a day eventually becomes a novel, and hand-washing contributes to an Olympic gold medal, your success is dependent on the small, consistent actions you take every day that bring you closer to your goals.

PASSION REQUIRES PRACTICE

It can be fun to daydream about what life will be like once you've built a successful practice. You'll have more control. You'll make more money. And, if you're doing it right, you'll have more time because you'll have a team of people working for you and your clients. You'll be like an entrepreneur who is working on their business, not in their business. Those are great outcomes to aim for, but the truth is that unless and until you learn to love (or at least like) the process of developing business, more control, money, and time—all important elements of autonomy—will remain out of reach.

When you learn to love the process required to reach a result, each day isn't drudgery; it's another opportunity for fulfillment. Realizing the fruits of developing more business becomes a goal, but not an obsession, because there is satisfaction in the everyday process of business development.

"It's the journey, not the destination" may sound like a trite cliché, but it's true. As those who have trained for and run marathons will attest, it's not the end of the 26.2-mile race that most remember, and are most proud of, over the long term. It's the hundreds of training miles that were logged in the months leading up to it. Those that try to run the race, but refuse to embrace the training, typically end up injured and disappointed even if they manage to cross the finish line. The satisfaction derives from the work, not the result. This principle applies even more acutely when it comes to the work we put into our careers because the stakes are so much higher.

Few of us have an inherent passion for business development—or "sales" as the rest of the world calls it. Few enter law school understanding that business development is a critical component of succeeding in private practice. Many decide to become a lawyer precisely because they abhor the idea of sales. But that doesn't mean you can't develop an interest, and perhaps even a passion, for business development.

The first step toward becoming passionate about something is developing an acumen for it. Hopefully this makes intuitive sense to you. The odds are that at some point in your life you've taken up a hobby—be it golf, running, knitting, or playing an instrument—that was difficult at first. You had an interest, but not necessarily a passion that led you to pursue it. You weren't particularly good at the hobby at first, and the activity you engaged in may not have been all that much fun until you became more competent at it. Eventually, as you honed your skills, you probably started enjoying it.

This concept—the important connection between hard work and satisfaction—is one that psychologist Mihaly Csikszentmihalyi studied in the early 1980s. Csikszentmihalyi conducted a series of studies with the intention of gaining an understanding of the psychological impact of common behaviors we engage in every day. One of the principal insights of his work was to show that depth generates meaning. According to Csikszentmihalyi, the best, most satisfying moments come when we stretch ourselves. Csikszentmihalyi popularized the term "flow state" to describe the feeling of effortlessness experienced by high achievers—from authors to athletes—operating at peak performance. But the psychological rewards of operating in a flow state don't come easily. Indeed, it's called "hard" work for a reason.

Any time you're learning a new skill, or building something worthwhile, it's hard. Enjoyment only comes after you've practiced enough to get good at something. When engaging in the work necessary to succeed in a challenging career, mastery is almost always a precursor to passion. And if you want to gain mastery over how to sell legal services, you have to (you guessed it!) practice, practice, practice. Successful lawyers manage to gain satisfaction in the work required to develop business, which allows them to do more of it—faster, better, and for longer periods of time—than their peers.

While many of your competitors are focused on putting in hours, you can rise above and build a greater passion for what you do by working systematically to develop the valuable skills required to create a book of business. By recognizing the fundamentals of high achievement, you'll have a leg up on those who are merely going through the motions. By creating the space and time necessary to engage in business development, you'll gain competence at it, and, someday, maybe even passion for it.

READY. FIRE. AIM.

Most lawyers are meticulous, detail-oriented, and analytical. Their "Type-A" perfectionism serves them well in the practice of law, but is often a hindrance when it comes to business development.

While the consequences of being imperfect in your legal work product can be harsh, imperfectionism is something you have to embrace in order to market and build a practice. You must take risks, go out on limbs, and take action without perfect knowledge of the outcome. When you're practicing law, your job is to de-risk situations for your client. When you're building a practice, you must act entrepreneurially and take calculated risks on your own behalf.

That's not to say that planning should be overlooked. Much of the ground this book has covered so far has addressed the importance of planning. It's critical to determine your direction before you start taking action. In an ideal world, lawyers setting out to build a practice would get ready (cast a vision), aim (set a goal and craft a plan), and fire (take action). In the real world, too many lawyers spend so much time aiming that they never fire at the target. They plan endlessly and never take action.

Successful people across different domains have a clear idea of what they want before they start taking action, but their tolerance for excessive planning is low. They have a bias toward action. They use the feedback they receive— good or bad—from the actions they take to determine what they'll do next. They view their plans as dynamic, subject to change based on the results of their actions, rather than set in stone. If you believe your plan must be perfect before you can take action, you never will.

When the Wright brothers set out to build an airplane, they faced stiff competition and seemingly insurmountable odds. Among their competitors was Samuel Pierpont Langley, who was well-connected with leaders in business and government. He was awarded a $50,000 grant from the U.S. War Department to build an airplane. He assembled a talented team and had access to technology and resources. The Wright brothers, on the other hand, were working with a ragtag team out of a small bicycle shop in North Carolina.

The Wright brothers ultimately won the race to build a working airplane because they prioritized action over planning. Unlike their competitors, who would spend enormous amounts of time and sums of money planning test flights, the Wright brothers tested frequently. After a failed flight, they would go back to their workshop, make tweaks, and test the plane again. Their competitors worked mostly in their heads. The Wright brothers took action and eventually took to the skies. Instead of endlessly aiming, they fired over and over, adjusting their approach along the way.

The Wright brothers succeeded because they learned and applied lessons learned from taking action. Their well-financed, well-connected competitors failed because they tried to eliminate risk by creating a more perfect plan.

Best-selling author and renowned business strategist Jim Collins urges prioritization of action over perpetual planning. In his book, *Good by Choice*, Collins explains that businesses (like people) have limited time and resources to work with. He asks readers to conjure a picture of themselves at sea, with a hostile vessel bearing down on their ship. There is a limited supply of ammunition and gunpowder available to fight off the attackers. A direct hit from a big cannonball is required to fend off the threat. But if panic sets in and a big cannonball is fired right away, it's likely to miss because there is no way to dial-in the correct aim. Most importantly, if a cannonball is fired first, there will be no gunpowder left for reloading.

If a smaller bullet is fired first, it is still likely to miss. But there will be plenty of gunpowder left to fire another one. Then another. With each successive shot, the aim improves until finally it's right on target. Through the experience of firing bullets, and dialing-in the aim, the remaining gunpowder can be used to fire off a big cannonball that hits its mark.

As you set out to market your practice and develop business, don't get caught up in endless cycles of planning. Conversely, when you do take action, don't go all-in on an approach without experimenting first. Take small actions, even imperfect ones, and assess the results. You'll learn from your successes, and, yes, your failures, and be able to refine your plan for the next set of actions you take. If you're the type of person who can't stop "aiming," try a "Ready, fire, aim!" approach instead.

BUILD NEW HABITS TO BUILD
A NEW IDENTITY

In a commencement speech to the 2014 University of Texas graduating class, Admiral William McRaven described how, during his training to become a Navy SEAL, instructors would come into his barracks bright and early each morning and the first thing they would do was inspect the beds of McRaven and other SEAL candidates. Their beds were expected to be up to Navy standards—corners square, covers pulled tight.

Navy SEALS are warriors. Part of becoming the type of person who can do the hard things required of a SEAL, McRaven explained, is making your bed to perfection, every morning, without fail. "It will give you a small sense of pride, and it will encourage you to do another task and another and another," McRaven said. "By the end of the day, that one task completed will have turned into many tasks completed. Making your bed will also reinforce the fact that little things in life matter. If you can't do the little things right, you will never do the big things right."[12]

Success in life, and as a lawyer, isn't determined by the boldness of your goals. You can't rely on willpower alone to keep you on track. To become the best version of yourself, you need to shift your focus from *what* you want to *who* you want to become.

While many people resist writing out their vision and goals, they find the exercise enjoyable once they do it. It's fun to dream about the future. It's an opportunity to envision the fruits of your labor. However, despite wanting the outcome, most fall short when it comes to execution.

Consider your own experiences. Have you ever gotten excited about achieving an outcome, such as running a marathon or writing a book? Perhaps you made progress toward your goal at first. Then, as is common, your inspiration may have waned and your progress sputtered.

The reason why it's so hard to make sustained progress toward a long-term vision is that we often try to achieve an outcome without changing our identities—our beliefs about who we are and want to become. Before you can do the difficult work to become someone new, you must form the fundamental belief that the change you seek is possible.

To illustrate the distinction between a focus on outcomes versus identity, consider the following two statements by a lawyer who desires to build a profitable book of business:

- I want to develop $500,000 in new business this year.
- I'm the type of person who devotes meaningful time to business development activity every single day.

The first is a worthy goal, but the second is a fundamental belief that makes the achievement of the goal possible. When you deeply believe something about yourself, your ability to act in accordance with that belief is no longer reliant upon willpower. Like brushing your teeth in the morning, it's simply what you do. You don't have to summon the willpower to brush your teeth, it's something you do on auto-pilot. It's a habit you formed because you're the type of person who has clean teeth.

As you begin the transformation from a lawyer who *wants* to develop business to one who *actually does,* it's critical that you begin to see yourself as the type of lawyer who consistently engages in business development activities. Your actions will then follow your beliefs. Every time you take action in accordance with your beliefs, you embody the identity you seek. When you fail to take action, you reinforce the belief that you're not capable or worthy of the outcome. Even if you're just getting started, you must act "as if" you are what you want to become.

For example, if you don't have clients of your own—but want to build a practice—you need to act as if you do. That doesn't mean you should mislead anyone about your past experience. What it does mean is that you must project confidence and engender trust that you're the right expert for the job when you have opportunities to interact with prospective clients. If you approach such conversations from a defensive posture, a prospect will sense your unease and be repelled by it. Your measured confidence will have the opposite effect. Confidence is attractive. When you believe in yourself, you create the conditions for others to believe in you, too.

Accordingly, transformation involves a two-stop process. First, define who you want to become. Second, reinforce your identity through consistent small actions. Do this, and before long business development will become a habitual part of your daily routine.

John Grisham believed he could become a writer. He reinforced that belief by acting as if he was a writer—he wrote at least one page every day. That's what writers do. As a result, he finished his first book. More importantly, through his belief in himself and his commitment to write every day, he established a writing habit that allowed him to go on to become a prolific international bestseller. Amateur writers wait for inspiration. Professionals write on a schedule. The same principle applies to a lawyer who wants to build a book of business.

Across domains, when people fail to achieve their goals,

it's typically because their desire for an end result is not matched by a commitment to do what it takes to get there. Everyone wants the result—the gold medal, the rewarding relationship, the book of business—but few are willing to put in the hard work that precedes the result. That is often due to a limiting belief that they're not capable or deserving of the outcomes they seek.

As you set out on your business development journey, focus less on achieving specific results and more on believing that you are the type of person who can achieve the things you desire. Achieving an outcome is a lagging indicator of success. Putting the work in on a consistent basis is a leading indicator. Start small and trust that results will come as you form a new identity. Your actions will follow your identity.

WORK BACKWARD TO MOVE FORWARD

Because success over the long term requires incremental action every day, it's necessary to define the everyday actions required to make progress. To accomplish this, you must first, as we've previously addressed, reduce your long-term vision to long-term goals that can realistically be achieved within a one-year timeframe. The next step is to deconstruct your big goals into a series of smaller ones.

The process of deconstructing a big goal into a smaller one helps in framing the work ahead as more approachable and doable. It reduces the propensity we all have to procrastinate or defer what needs to get done because we simply don't know where to begin. Instead of focusing on a deadline to perform by, it's important to establish a schedule to operate by. Put simply, goal deconstruction transforms a desire into an actionable plan.

Let's say you're a third-year associate and your long-term vision is to make partner at your law firm. That means you have approximately five years to work with. Accordingly, you will need to make a certain amount of progress in the next year to be on track to realize your five-year vision. For example, developing relationships with prospective clients and referral sources takes time. A high level of trust must be established before business development opportunities will arise. It often takes years to establish relationships that ultimately turn into new business. You will need to begin cultivating relationships now for them to lead to new business later.

You must think of the next five years as a series of five dominoes: You must knock down the first in order to topple the second, and so on.

Consider the alternative. If you don't make significant progress in the coming year, you'll fall behind and be forced to get more work done within a smaller window of time later. Your deadline won't change, just the amount of time you have to work with. Next thing you know, you will be a seventh-year associate who is being told that you need a book of business to make partner. You will be scrambling furiously to catch up.

Except you can't. There's no time. You still have hefty billable hour requirements. And there are only 168 hours in a week. Only in the rearview mirror can you now see that you had to start sooner.

This won't be *your* fate, however, because now you know that you need to cast aside the type of short-term thinking that prevents others from making long-term progress. Using the SMART goal framework, you will establish a clear and actionable one-year goal that will put you on the path to realize your vision. You will recognize that, to get where you need to be in one year, you will have to take action this month. A month passes quickly, so you will have a plan in place to make progress this week. And since you're committed to making progress this week, you will take some small action in furtherance of your long-term priorities today.

See how this works? You're capable of achieving extraordinary results way out in the future. But actually doing so is contingent upon taking action every day. It's the steady consistency, not the episodic intensity, of business development effort that matters.

Making progress on long-term objectives is all about deconstructing your goals into specific action steps within the constraints of allotted time. Work backward to understand the component parts of your big goal, establish a series of smaller goals based on that understanding, and then create a plan that will keep you working diligently and moving forward. You should deconstruct your big goal to the point where you have a clear understanding of the appropriate action you should be taking today— at this very moment—to be on the right path.

Nick Saban, coach of the University of Alabama football team, has won multiple national championships. Throughout each season, he urges his players not to fixate on the future, but rather to take the next appropriate action in the present moment. The team's goal every year is to win the national championship. Saban's directive is to win the moment. Here's how he describes his approach, which is called The Process: "Don't think about the national championship. Think about what you need to do in this drill, on this play, in this moment. That's the process: Let's think about what we can do today, the task at hand."

Whether you're a lawyer or a linebacker, if you win today, you're one step closer to winning in the future. When you focus on the process, the results will follow.

Think about it this way: The goals you set are waypoints on the road to realizing your long-term vision. Goals determine your direction. The systems you put in place for action are what determine your progress. As best-selling author James Clear wrote in his book *Atomic Habits: An Easy & Proven Way of Building Good Habits and Breaking Bad Ones,* "You don't rise to the level of your goals. You fall to the level of your systems." Most lawyers have the same goals. Those who succeed merely have better systems. By deconstructing your big goal into a system for daily action, you'll set yourself up to realize the compounding returns of incremental progress.

To create a system based on the deconstruction of a big goal into smaller ones, start with the end in mind. Let's say that one of your SMART goals for the year is to publish one thought-leadership article every month on a website or in a trade publication that is frequently read by members of your target market. The purpose of such a goal is to establish yourself as an expert within an industry niche.

To accomplish this goal, you will need to consider the steps involved in creating and publishing thought-leadership articles, which include things like topic ideation, research, writing, editing, and developing editorial relationships. If you want to reach your audience, you'll also need to promote your content—in today's noisy world, it won't promote itself.

After establishing a goal to publish 12 thought-leadership articles over the course of the year, you'll need to deconstruct that big goal into 12 smaller ones—each involving the creation of one piece of content per month. You should then allocate the time necessary to work on the various aspects of content creation over the course of each month.

For example, week one of each month could be spent on topic ideation and research. Week two could involve writing. Week three, editing. And week four is when you could pitch your article to an editor. Following the publication of your article, you'll want to schedule time to promote it on social media and elsewhere. On each day, during each week, you will need to set aside the appropriate amount of time necessary to stay on track for your monthly goal, which will allow you to achieve your yearly goal.

Whatever your goal is, you need to remain consistent. Saving a bit of money right now won't make you wealthy tomorrow. But starting to save today greatly increases your odds of building wealth in the future. The same is true of business development. You may not notice the impact of the small actions you take on a particular day, but over the course of months and years, your daily actions will compound into significant business development gains.

Chapter Summary

——

Every big goal is made up of a series of smaller ones. To accomplish your long-term goals, you must break them down into a series of small and specific action steps. When it comes to business development, the best way to achieve your goals is to make the activities that drive new business habitual. Business development doesn't happen in one fell swoop—It's the consistency of your actions that matters most. Small actions, done every day, compound into big long-term results.

COACHING NOTE:
Create a Weekly Plan

When you set annual goals, it can be difficult to know what actions to take on a daily or weekly basis that will move you closer to achieving your goals. Use the Weekly Planner available at **www.productivitypivot.com** to help you deconstruct your long-term goal into actions you can take every day.

PART 2:

THE
DAILY
PRACTICE

4

Sell Yourself One Hour Every Day

"Never leave 'till tomorrow which you can do today."

– BENJAMIN FRANKLIN

W hile Charlie would go on to become one of the richest people on earth, he started his career the way most lawyers do, with one eye on the clock making sure he recorded each minute he spent toiling away for his clients.

Charlie grew up in Nebraska and studied math at the University of Michigan before dropping out to join the U.S. Army Air Corps following the attacks at Pearl Harbor. Following his military service during World War II, he turned his attention to his career.

His father was a lawyer, as was his grandfather, so he decided to follow in their footsteps. He applied to Harvard Law School, his father's alma mater, and was initially rejected because he had not completed his undergraduate degree. After some cajoling by a family friend named Roscoe Pound (who happened to be a former dean of Harvard Law School), Charlie was admitted and later graduated *magna cum laude* from Harvard Law School in 1948.

After graduation, he moved to California with his family and began practicing law as an associate at a law firm. Early in his legal career, Charlie came to an important realization that would help set him on a path toward massive success—as a lawyer and then as an investor. He recognized that he was spending all of his time working on behalf of his clients. As a result, he was doing little to serve the person he came to realize was his most important client: himself.

For Charlie Munger, who went on to co-found powerhouse law firm Munger, Tolles & Olson LLP, and later became a billionaire businessman as Warren Buffett's partner in Berkshire Hathaway, the realization that he was his own most important client led him to adopt a daily practice as a young lawyer that became critical to his long-term success. He began "selling" himself the most important hour of his day—every day, first thing in the morning—and he used the time to work on personal and professional development. He wasn't satisfied with his circumstances, so he decided to work for himself—one hour every day—to improve them.

In an interview he gave for his authorized biography, *The Snowball: Warren Buffett and the Business of Life,* Buffett recounts Munger's approach: "Charlie, as a very young lawyer, was probably getting $20 an hour. He thought to himself, 'Who's my most valuable client?' And he decided it was himself. So he decided to sell himself an hour each day. He did it early in the morning, working on these construction projects and real estate deals. Everybody should do this, be the client, and then work for other people, too, and sell yourself an hour a day."

Most lawyers think the path to success lies in devoting as much time as possible to working for paying clients. However, as Munger learned and Buffett observed, the best investment you'll ever make is selling yourself one hour of your time every day.

Massive long-term success comes from making daily, incremental progress. As Munger advised in his book, *Poor Charlie's Almanack: The Wit and Wisdom of Charles T. Munger,* "Spend each day trying to be a little wiser than you were when you woke up. Day by day, and at the end of the day—if you live long enough—like most people, you will get out of life what you deserve."

If you find the idea of carving out an hour every day to engage in business development activities unrealistic, you're not alone. Despite the fact that one hour constitutes merely ten percent of most lawyers' time each workday, they view an hour-per-day approach as unsustainable. What's unsustainable, however, is the sporadic, frenetic alternative.

Many lawyers treat business development the same way most of us think about bathing suit season—we work hard at it when we need to. When spring break approaches, we hit the gym. When October rolls around, we start raiding our kids' Halloween candy.

In the case of business development, when lawyers are slow at work, they ramp up their business development efforts, and then tamp things down when business picks up. Legal business development becomes a rollercoaster; a cycle of ups and downs that creates stress and uncertainty. Action is driven by urgency, not strategic planning.

The problem with a sporadic approach to business development is that lawyers often overreact and overcorrect when times get slow. They engage in a bluster of business development activity that brings in work—often more work than they can handle from clients who are a poor fit. Then they stop all business development activity to focus on the work they have. Then... you guessed it. The cycle repeats.

Lawyers who find themselves riding this up-and-down cycle typically lack an understanding of the sustained level of business development activity that is required to keep themselves, and others in their firm, busy on a consistent basis.

The key to business development success is to do the right thing, the right way, at the right time by forming a business development habit and investing in yourself every day. By forming a business development habit, you will ward off the procrastination that tends to creep in when client work gets busy. You'll avoid the temptation to put off business development until it becomes imperative when things slow down.

It takes discipline to spend an hour connecting with prospects or writing a thought-leadership article when a brief is due at the end of the day. However, having the discipline to act when you have the urge to defer is what separates rain-makers from order-takers. It's also what leads to a long-term business development habit. The more you do something, the more success you'll have at it, and the more success you have, the more you'll want to do the thing that led to it. By selling yourself an hour every day, you'll create a positive cycle of business development activity that will continue to build momentum. By engaging in thoughtful and strategic business development activities, done at a specific time every day, it will become automatic and won't require large expenditures of energy and willpower.

Consistent procrastination, on the other hand, may feel good in the short term, but is detrimental over the long term. In a study published in *Psychological Science* in 1997, researchers rated college students on a predefined scale of procrastination and then tracked their academic performance, stress, and general health throughout the semester.[13] In the short term, students who were prone to procrastination realized some benefits. They had lower levels of stress compared to others, as they put off their work to pursue more enjoyable activities. Over the long term, the costs of procrastination significantly outweighed the temporary benefits. Procrastinators earned lower grades than more proactive students and experienced higher cumulative amounts of stress and illness.

Billing endless hours while procrastinating when it comes to business development activities is a short-term pitfall. A big billable day may give you a satisfying rush fueled by a release of dopamine. Because you like the way that feels, you'll do your best to replicate the experience. Assuming there is plenty of work to do at your firm, clocking more billables is simple. You just have to do the work that's in front of you. While legal work isn't easy, its deadline-driven nature eliminates, or at least reduces, the risk of procrastination.

If you're just getting started with business development, it's unlikely to be a satisfying experience at first. Let's face it, it's going to be a while before you're bringing in clients, so you can't count on neurotransmitters like dopamine to keep yourself going. What is required is discipline, at least at the beginning. By giving in to your short-term desires, such as by prioritizing billable hours over everything else, you'll pay the long-term price of never achieving a sense of autonomy in the practice of law.

Yes, there are some short-term trade-offs that you may have to accept if you commit to daily business development. Don't worry, they're worth it. As Charlie Munger said, "I have always wanted to improve what I do, even if it reduces my income in any given year." By carving out an hour of time every day for business development activities, you may earn less this year, but you'll gain much more in the end.

"BUT I DON'T HAVE THE TIME"

The process I use to coach attorneys to become more consistent and successful at business development is based on the principles addressed in this book.

First, cast a bold vision for the future,

Second, establish SMART goals that will put you on a path to realize your vision.

Third, deconstruct your goals into an actionable plan with enough specificity that it allows you to identify the next appropriate step to take to be on track for achieving your goals.

Fourth, start taking action—ideally one hour's worth every day.

Working through steps one, two, and three typically elicits a great deal of enthusiasm from my clients. Despite the fact that one hour represents only four percent of someone's time each day, step four is where most people get hung up.

In rock climbing, the most difficult part of every climb is called the crux. It's the spot on the rock face at which most climbers fail. When it comes to business development, the crux is the point at which a lawyer has to commit to daily action.

The first and most important mountain to climb is a mental one. It's your brain, not the rest of your body, that's getting in the way of your taking action. It's trying to protect you from discomfort. But to succeed at business development, it's necessary to get comfortable with experiencing discomfort.

The skills attorneys must develop to build a practice can only be acquired through observation, trial, and error—especially error. Yes, business development is mostly about failure, which is one of the main reasons that many lawyers, who by nature are competitive and like to win, and also tend to be averse to risk, don't relish the business development process.

If you talk to successful professionals who consistently engage in business development, they will tell you that they lose the sale far more often than they win it. But there's a bright side to losing. With every failure comes the chance to learn and adapt. Successful lawyers are not discouraged by unsuccessful efforts. They see each "failure" as an opportunity to get better and draw lessons from the experience that help guide their future actions. This mindset shift leads to more business development activity, not less, and ultimately more success.

Accordingly, it's important to recognize that as you begin your business development journey, your brain will start constructing obstacles in your way in the form of beliefs you have about yourself and your circumstances. You may find yourself thinking, "I'm not good enough," or "I'm not disciplined enough." These are limiting beliefs that cap your potential and establish self-imposed boundaries that prevent you from accomplishing big things. Your beliefs dictate your behaviors, and, therefore, determine your future.

In my coaching practice, when I challenge my clients to

sell themselves one hour every day, the limiting belief I hear most often is: "I just don't have the time." Lawyers suggest they can't find the time to focus on business development because, "Things are crazy right now, but should settle down once this case wraps up." But things never settle down. Client work never goes away. There's always another case on the horizon. And from senior partners to junior associates, it's the same refrain: "There's no time."

All you have to do is look around to understand that "I don't have the time" is a self-constructed obstacle. There are likely lawyers in your firm, and certainly lawyers outside of it, who have cast aside their limiting beliefs to prioritize time every day for business development.

With rare exceptions, anyone who is accomplishing great things and building a great practice is not engaging in a sporadic, scattershot approach to business development. The people who are getting ahead have the same 168 hours a week that you do, yet they find the time to serve their clients and themselves. Their success is a manifestation of the principle that two people can experience the same circumstances—in this case, a perceived lack of time—yet respond to them completely differently.

Have you ever audited how you spend your time each day? As a busy lawyer, it probably feels like time is always a resource that's in short supply. But if you look closely, you'll find that there is enough time to do what needs to be done each day—such as a dedicated hour of business development.

Be brutally honest with yourself: Are you spending your time working, or are you fitting in work between distractions? Distractions at the office come in many forms. Relentless email. Mind-numbing meetings. Chatty colleagues. Facebook. LinkedIn. Phone calls. Administrative responsibilities that you should be delegating to others.

Ever go on the Internet to check out "one quick thing," and emerge from a daze 20 minutes later wondering what the hell just happened? You get the idea. In fact, that "minute or two" you spend online checking Instagram is costing you much more.

According to a study conducted by Gloria Mark, who studies digital distraction at the University of California, Irvine, it takes an average of 23 minutes and 15 seconds to return to your original task after an interruption. That 30 seconds spent chatting with your colleague who popped in your office? It just cost you 25 minutes of productivity.

Distractions have real implications. If you're frequently getting distracted, then you're probably working in 15-minute increments (if you're lucky) throughout the day, getting little accomplished, and resorting to beginning your real work after 6 p.m., when distractions finally die down. Not only do distractions crush productivity, but they can impact you emotionally as well by increasing stress and affecting your mood. They're likely getting in the way of your ability to engage in business development, too.

Even if you've limited or eliminated distractions from your work day, you still may find yourself feeling perpetually pressed for time, and pushing off business development as a result. Nature abhors a vacuum, and so do billable hours.

In 1955, British historian Cyril Northcote Parkinson wrote an essay in *The Economist* in which he described a phenomenon that would come to be known as "Parkinson's Law." He wrote: "Work expands so as to fill the time available for its completion." In other words, if something must be done in a day, it will get done in a day. If something must be done in a year, it will get done in a year.

If you believe that achieving success as a lawyer requires

you to spend all of your time each day billing hours on client work, then it will. It's Parkinson's Law of being a lawyer. However, Parkinson's Law works the other way around, too. If you spend an hour a day developing business—an hour that you would have otherwise spent billing hours—you will be more focused and efficient at getting your client work done during the remainder of the day. I'm not suggesting that your law firm doesn't care about how many hours you bill. But over the long term, it will care more about you making a bigger impact on the bottom line by building a profitable book of business. Billable hours may keep you employed, but having great clients will get you promoted to partner and increase your profit-sharing.

Accordingly, if you're not rigorous about blocking time in your schedule to engage in business development activities, your mind will default to what comes naturally to most lawyers: billing more hours. The practice of law is deadline-driven. Your clients and your supervising lawyers within your firm set deadlines for you. It's time to start setting some for yourself.

All of this is to say that, in most cases, lack of time is not the issue. Successful lawyers prioritize the time necessary to do the difficult tasks required to achieve their desired outcomes. They avoid distractions in order to focus on what's most important. They don't blame their lack of progress on being too busy. In fact, the busiest lawyers are typically those who spend the most time developing business, because they have to manage the practices they're building. If they can prioritize time for business development, you can, too. In the words of the author H. Jackson Brown, "Don't say you don't have enough time. You have exactly the same number of hours per day that were given to Helen Keller, Pasteur, Michelangelo, Mother Teresa, Leonardo da Vinci, Thomas

Jefferson, and Albert Einstein."

Like a good trial lawyer, you need to cross-examine the limiting belief that you don't have time to focus on business development. In his book, *Why Your Life Sucks...and What You Can Do About It,* Alan Cohen suggests an approach that may resonate with you: "Imagine two lawyers in a courtroom inside your head. One is arguing for your possibilities and you achieving your goals. The other is arguing for your limits and why you don't deserve what you want. Who will win? The lawyer you pay the most. The way you pay these lawyers, however, is not with money; it is with your attention."

Indeed, achieving anything meaningful requires that you believe you're capable of such achievement, because our actions conform to our beliefs. Seventy years ago, everyone believed that running a mile in under four minutes was physically impossible, and so it was. Then Roger Bannister stepped forward and did it. A few weeks later, John Landy followed. Within three years, 16 runners had accomplished the "impossible" feat of running a four-minute mile.

If you don't believe it's possible to devote one hour every day to build a successful practice, it won't be. But if that's what you're telling yourself, you're ignoring evidence to the contrary. Around the same time that Roger Bannister broke the four-minute mile barrier, Charlie Munger figured out that the secret to getting ahead was focusing on what was most important to himself. Countless other lawyers—some of whom are likely working at your law firm—are following in Munger's footsteps, and succeeding at building a practice. Will you be one of them?

If you're not devoting time and attention to your own most important priorities, you'll spend your career working on someone else's. However, if you cross-examine your limiting beliefs about the scarcity of time and expose them for what they are—merely a story you tell yourself—you will open the door to success. Next, you need to step through it.

Chapter Summary

———

When a lawyer fails to consistently engage in business development activities, it's almost never because they don't know what to do. In almost all cases, it's because they failed to set aside sufficient time to make forward progress. Everything else—primarily billable hours—gets in the way. Instead of prioritizing the time for themselves, lawyers spend their time working on someone else's priorities.

Lawyers who succeed in building practices adopt the mindset that they are their own most important client. And they affirm that belief by selling themselves one hour of their time every day. Blocking off an hour of their time each day allows them to consistently work on their goals. Like other lawyers, they're pressed for time, but they don't use their busyness as an excuse to not put in the work. They don't succumb to limiting beliefs about the scarcity of time. They view the one hour of time they sell to themselves as the most important part of the day, and they use the remainder of their time, attention, and energy to effectively serve their outside clients.

COACHING NOTE:
Baby Steps

The reason most people fail when trying to change their behaviors is that they bite off more than they can chew. When someone wants to lose weight, they start by going to the gym seven days a week. Predictably, they can't keep up that pace, quickly fall off the wagon, and then quit exercising because they feel like a failure. Don't fall into this trap when setting out to devote time to business development every day. Your goal should be to work up to spending one hour every day on business development—not necessarily to start spending one hour from day one. Instead, try 15 or 20 minutes per day for a month. For most, that's a more manageable schedule to start with. Increase the amount of time you spend as you begin making other productivity gains throughout your day which allow you to buy more time for business development.

Focus on First
Things First

"Things that matter most must never be at
the mercy of things that matter least."
– JOHANN WOLFGANG VON GOETHE

W hile Part 1 of this book focuses on helping
you to define what you want out of your
career through a process of casting a clear
vision, setting goals that move you closer
to that vision, and deconstructing your goals into a plan
for daily action, in Part 2 we're diving into what is required
to make daily business development progress. That process
starts with selling yourself an hour of your time every day.
The next step involves determining what you *should* do, not

merely what you *can* do, during the hour you've set aside for yourself. Even if you're clear on your objectives, if you try to tackle everything at once, you'll end up working hard but will make little progress.

Most lawyers are smart, highly capable individuals who become adept at juggling a number of different legal matters at once. Few lawyers have the luxury of working on only one case at a time. There's a difference, however, between having multiple responsibilities and trying to work on multiple tasks at the same time.

There's an old Russian proverb that states: "If you chase two rabbits, you will not catch either one." As much as we might like to believe that we are capable of multitasking, we can't. At least we can't if we want to be effective. Multitasking, which means working on two or more things at the same time, is often heralded as a high mark of productivity. The truth is that most of us are multitasking ourselves into insignificance.

Clifford Nass, a Stanford sociologist who was one of the first academics to study the effects of multitasking, conducted a study in 2009 through which he found that those who frequently engage in multitasking underperform on every measure relative to infrequent multitaskers. Nass argues that those who can't stop themselves from trying to do more than one thing at once are "suckers for irrelevancy."[14] Not only that, but multitasking actually makes us dumber while we try to engage in it. Research from the University of London found that our IQ drops by 5 to 15 points when we multitask.[15]

Sophie Leroy, a business school professor at the University of Minnesota, also conducted a study on multitasking and found that people are less productive when they switch from one task to another, instead of focusing on one thing at a time. It's pretty easy to understand why it's not a good idea to work on an important brief or deal document while at the same time sitting in on a conference call. However, you may be surprised to learn that jumping back and forth between a legal brief and conference calls throughout the day—no matter how much focus is applied to each task independently—also undermines results. Leroy's work proves that you'll hamper your productivity if you frequently toggle between tasks, even if you only work on one task at a time.

Our minds are not computers. We can't seamlessly transition from one task to another without carryover effects. When we switch from writing a brief to participating on a conference call and then back to writing the brief, we're carrying mental baggage with us from the previous task as we attempt to move forward to the new one. Leroy calls this baggage "attention residue."[16]

Multitasking happens because of a lack of discipline. Despite knowing that it would be more efficient to work on one thing at a time until it makes strategic sense to switch to the next one, many lawyers default to bouncing between emails, documents, and browser windows, and their productivity suffers. It also results from a lack of focus. If you don't plan out the logical sequence of work, in order of its priority, it's impossible to know what to do next—so you give everything equal billing.

Trying to multitask your way through your day is deleterious to both your legal work and your efforts to develop business. Even if you carve out an hour of time for business development, it will be wasted unless you have a clear understanding of what you should be doing during that time. That understanding must be gained in advance, through planning and preparation, not in the moment.

An hour goes by quickly. If you're trying to act in the

moment, and not in accordance with a clear and predetermined plan of action, then, as professor Nass would say, you'll end up multitasking yourself into irrelevancy. On the other hand, those who act in furtherance of a plan spend their time creating thought-leadership content, setting up meetings with prospects, and working on long-term, high-impact projects like books and speeches.

They get things done because they know the substance and sequence of the actions they must take. They know what to do next because they've taken the time to distinguish between that which is important and that which seems important but is merely urgent.

BE LIKE IKE

Dwight "Ike" Eisenhower was a five-star general in the U.S. Army and served as the Supreme Commander of the Allied Forces in Europe during World War II. He was responsible for planning and executing invasions of North Africa, France, and Germany. He also served two terms as the 34th President of the United States. As president, he signed the Civil Rights Bill of 1957, helped establish America's interstate highway system, negotiated an end to the Korean War, and supported the launch of the NASA program, among other accomplishments. Following his presidency, he went on to serve as president of Columbia University and as the first Supreme Commander of NATO.

Needless to say, Eisenhower was a busy guy. It's no surprise, then, that his productivity and time-management practices are studied today. His time was always limited yet he consistently accomplished his objectives. He was bombarded with distractions and urgent demands but never lost sight of his long-term vision. His example is worth studying.

Eisenhower created a framework for processing and prioritizing the immense amount of decisions he had to make, and tasks he had to perform, as a wartime leader and then as president. The "Eisenhower Matrix," as his framework is now called, consists of four quadrants.

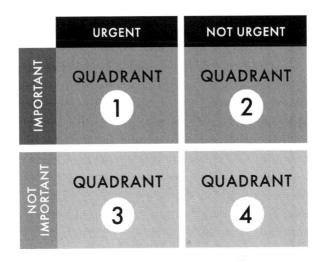

Quadrant 1. Eisenhower once said, "What is important is seldom urgent and what is urgent is seldom important." Nonetheless, a sense of urgency drives much of what lawyers must do on a daily basis. Legal work is deadline-driven *and* important, so a great deal of your daily to-do list will reside in Quadrant 1. Most of your time each day should be spent working on Quadrant 1 tasks that allow you to meet deadlines imposed by clients, courts, regulations, and rules of civil procedure… *but not all of your time.*

Quadrant 2. There is work that must be done that is important but not urgent. This is work that can be deferred without any negative short-term repercussions. However, it shouldn't be deferred, because there are long-term consequences to putting it off. Work that falls into Quadrant 2 is that which allows you to move forward on your long-term vision and goals.

Quadrant 3. There are time-sensitive tasks that must get done but are not particularly important. Quadrant 3 tasks are typically more administrative in nature, like logging timekeeping entries, booking travel, or responding to unimportant emails. These are tasks that typically can be done by someone else. In chapter 6, we will discuss how to delegate urgent but not important work effectively.

Quadrant 4. Tasks that are neither urgent nor important should never appear on a lawyer's calendar or to-do list, but often still do. Have you ever accepted a lunch invitation or meeting request from someone and regretted it the moment you said yes? You didn't need a custom-tailored suit or a whole-life insurance policy, but you felt compelled to say yes to the salesperson's invitation out of a sense of guilt or because you lacked clarity about how you should be spending your time. In the process, you gave someone else an hour of your time in furtherance of their priorities and to the detriment of your own. We will address the importance of saying no in Chapter 6 as well.

The Eisenhower Matrix is effective because it forces us to start thinking about time qualitatively and not merely quantitatively. The question is not *whether* you have the time to do something, but rather *should* you be doing it at all. Are you spending all your time checking urgent items off your to-do list, or are you setting aside the time required to dig in on the important work that will have a meaningful long-term impact?

For most lawyers, assuming they're spending, on average,

10 hours at the office each day, approximately 80 percent of their time should be spent working on Quadrant 1 client work. Provided they are working diligently and limiting distractions, eight hours a day (with a few more mixed in on nights and weekends every once in a while) should allow them to meet their client demands and billable hour requirements. That leaves an hour for Quadrant 3 activities, such as lunch and administrative responsibilities. What's left? You guessed it: one hour of time to spend on important, long-term Quadrant 2 priorities.

How you spend your time each day will largely be dictated by deadlines and client demands. That's an inevitable part of being a lawyer. Unless you sell yourself one hour of your time every day to work on that which is important but not urgent, all your time will be spent serving others. It is only during windows of time set aside to work for yourself that you will have the freedom—the autonomy—to work on business development activities that everyone knows are important but few prioritize.

DO IT FIRST THING

I grew up playing whatever sport was in season. I went on to play baseball in college. My days in college were structured around games, practices, and workouts, and I had to fit in classes and studying during the time that was left over. During law school, on a typical day, I would attend classes for three hours a day and study for three more. There was plenty of time left over to hit the gym for an hour. Throughout my early years, staying physically fit wasn't a problem because engaging in physical activity was a routine part of my day.

At the age of 25, I started working at a large and demanding law firm. My first day on the job was six days after the 9/11 terrorist attacks, and I was working in the corporate bankruptcy department at my firm. I had a crushing workload. When I wasn't at my desk, I was feeling anxious because I had so much to do. When I was at my desk, I was stressed because I didn't always know what I was doing.

Before I knew it, I was 30 years old, and the physically fit, youthful version of myself was a distant memory. I had transformed into an inactive desk jockey, and had the physique to prove it. I never lost the desire to stay physically active, but couldn't seem to find the time or muster the discipline to get to the gym.

Because I was stressed about work, I would race into the office every morning. I figured that if I could get into the office early and dive into my work, I could get caught up or even get ahead. Of course, I never did. There was always another wave coming after the one that had just crashed on top of me. Almost every day, at least during the early stages of my career, I had the intention of going to the gym after work. Then the intensity of each day got the better of me, sapped whatever energy I had, and more often than not (okay, almost always) I would default to picking up a beer after work rather than a barbell.

It was only after my first daughter was born that things changed. I always knew the path I was on—dominated by work and devoid of self-care—was headed in the wrong direction, but having a child brought this fact into stark relief. If I wanted to be there for her, I had to take care of myself, which meant I had to prioritize myself.

The solution was pretty simple and obvious: Instead of repeating past behaviors, which involved forming a weak intention every day to exercise after work, I committed to working out first thing in the morning, three days per week. I'd lay out my clothes and put my shoes by the door the night before, and force myself to get to an exercise class by 6 a.m. I hated it at first, mostly because I was so out of shape, but before long I started experiencing positive results. The weight started coming off, and before long, three days a week became four, then five.

I started feeling and looking better, and I had more energy during the day. As a result, my legal work improved and stress levels lessened. I found magic in the early morning.

At that point in my career, I was running my own law firm. For the first time, the burden of bringing in new business fell squarely on my back. Previously, I had been practicing as an associate at large firms working on complex corporate restructuring matters generated by other lawyers in the firm. Fresh off my revelation that great things can happen first thing in the morning, I started to work on business development tactics at the beginning of each day.

In truth, I had no other choice. If I had not prioritized business development, there would have been no revenue coming in to keep the lights on, let alone to pay myself. Some time later, however, as business started coming in more consistently and I got busy with client work, I abandoned my early morning business development routine.

Inevitably, things started slipping into an up-and-down cycle of busy periods, during which I would focus on billable hours, and slow ones, during which I had to shift back to business development and chase down more work. After a couple of nausea-inducing roller coaster rides, I realized that the problem wasn't the intensity of my effort—I went all-in on business development when I had to—it was the inconsistency of that effort.

Having been sufficiently chastened, I went back to my

old routine of doing business development first thing in the morning, and then fitting in everything else throughout the day. Without knowing it at the time, I was adhering to Charlie Munger's admonishment to "sell" myself an hour of my time every day. And it worked. I no longer had to periodically count on a huge wave of work coming in to keep the office busy. The daily ripples were enough. I came to realize that productivity didn't mean getting more things done in frenetic bursts, but rather getting important things done consistently.

For me, and I'm betting for you, too, the best way to get important things done is to do them first thing in the morning.

The fact that it's better to do meaningful work like business development early in the day is a no-brainer. If you've been working all day in a stressful profession such as the practice of law, by evening your brain is fried, your productivity sagging, and you almost certainly won't be doing your best work. When you're tired, it's easy to defer work that is important but not necessarily urgent to the next day. And aren't you always tired at the end of a long day of doing legal work?

Discipline is not an infinite resource. It depletes throughout the day. If you're running a long race every day that requires discipline, caffeine, or some other catalyst to keep going at the same fast pace, then you'll always be falling behind as the day drags on like an overly aggressive marathoner who "bonks" at mile 16.

Don't save your most important work for the end of the day. And if you want to gain autonomy and realize your long-term vision, then business development is your most important work. Do it first thing, when your mind and body are fresh.

If you do the most important thing first each day, then you'll always get something important done. Like a Navy SEAL who makes his bed upon waking up, you will create a positive sense of momentum that will carry you through the rest of your day.

If you defer business development work in the hope of fitting it in at some later point in the day, you'll be relying on willpower to get it done. However, as researchers found when studying a parole board considering the fate of Israeli prisoners, relying on willpower to get important things done is a risky proposition.[17]

The study found that board members were far more likely to grant prisoners parole at the start of the day and after lunch breaks. The board granted parole in nearly 65 percent of cases at the beginning of the day, but as the day dragged on and parole board members became fatigued from making decision after decision, the likelihood of a prisoner being granted a release dropped to nearly zero.

As each day wore on, the board members began to experience what is called "decision fatigue." When faced with too many decisions, people are more likely to opt for the default choice. In the cases being considered by the Israeli parole board, the default decision was the denial of parole.

Busy lawyers suffer from decision fatigue, too. Lawyers are forced to make difficult decisions all day, every day. All those decisions come at a cost. They deplete willpower throughout the day. And when your willpower gets depleted, business development is often the first thing to get deferred from your to-do list. When you're feeling tired, it's easier to work on someone else's priority than it is to summon the willpower to pursue your own.

To get ahead at work, you need to put yourself first. Your

clients can come in a close second. But you need to reserve your most valuable hour of each day for yourself. And for most, that hour comes first thing each morning. According to psychologist Ron Friedman, the early morning is the critical time to maximize your productivity. "Typically, we have a window of about three hours where we're really, really focused. We're able to have some strong contributions in terms of planning, in terms of thinking, in terms of speaking well," Friedman told the *Harvard Business Review*.[18]

Not only is your willpower strongest immediately following sleep[19], your mind is most active and readily creative[20] in the first few hours of each day as well. You will be your most efficient- and effective-self if you do business development first thing. Don't fall into the trap of trying to fit in an hour of business development time when it's convenient—because it never is. To work at your peak level of performance on your most important priority, schedule time for it first thing in the morning.

Chapter Summary

———

To be productive and efficient, and to devote sufficient time to business development, it is necessary to distinguish between urgent priorities, which tend to garner the most attention, and important priorities that aren't necessarily urgent. You may not feel a sense of urgency about engaging in business development activities on a particular day when you have urgent client matters to address, but if you don't remain consistent with business development, you'll get into a habit of procrastinating when it comes to your most important long-term priority.

The Eisenhower Matrix is a tool that allows you to categorize and visualize the qualitative nature of your work. By distinguishing between urgent and important work, you can focus more time, attention, and energy on the work that matters. You'll stop giving all work equal billing.

When lawyers are unclear about their priorities, they tend to multitask. They try to work on more than one task at once—such as answering emails while participating on conference calls—and they bounce between tasks throughout the day. They start a project, get distracted by incoming emails, and then try to pick up the original task later in the day. Because their minds are always in transition, they have a hard time bringing their best to any particular task. A better approach, whenever possible, is to work on a task until it is complete before moving on to the next one.

Once you have a handle on your most important priority, and for almost every lawyer, business development is most important, you should work on it for one hour first thing each morning. Take advantage of the most valuable hour of your day, when your mind is fresh, your willpower is high, and distractions are at a minimum. This will allow you to get your most important work done.

COACHING NOTE:
Prioritize Your Work Using the
Eisenhower Matrix

Amid the fast pace of the practice of law, it can be hard to step back and assess the nature of the work you do. When stress is high, and deadlines are looming, everything feels equally urgent and important. But it's not. The Eisenhower Matrix is a tool that can help you evaluate whether you're spending your finite time and attention on work that really matters. Visit **www.productivitypivot.com** to download the Eisenhower Matrix Worksheet and use it to categorize your work in each of the Eisenhower Matrix's four quadrants. By doing so, you'll get a handle on what you should be focused on, and, as we'll discuss in chapter 6, what you can delegate to others and eliminate altogether.

The 60-Minute
Daily Sprint

"The time that leads to mastery is dependent
on the intensity of our focus."

– ROBERT GREENE

n his book, *On Writing: A Memoir of the Craft*, Stephen King wrote, "Amateurs sit and wait for inspiration, the rest of us just get up and go to work." In the first five chapters of this book, we addressed the philosophical and strategic principles that underpin effective productivity. We explored the distinction Dwight Eisenhower drew between the urgent and the important. We discussed Charlie Munger's framework for selling yourself one hour of your time every day. You have the mental models you need to succeed. Let's now get more tactical. As King suggests, let's get up and go to work.

Your objective should be to make incremental progress every day. You don't need to do significantly more business development work than your competitors. You just need to be marginally better, smarter, and more diligent to gain a significant advantage. In every city of any size, swarms of lawyers fight for business within niche markets. Over time, a small number of competitors come to dominate. There is not an even distribution of rewards. Those at the top generate most of the profits. They win in winner-takes-all markets.

In the practice of law, those perceived to be at the top of their fields in particular areas of practice are on the shortlist for most new engagements in their respective market niches. They command high fees. They get to pick and choose. Often, they are only slightly more skilled—if at all—than the multitude of other undifferentiated lawyers who are left to compete for lower-margin work on the basis of price. Like a sprinter who runs a mere 1/10th of a second faster than their competitors, the lawyer who establishes a razor-thin advantage gains almost all the rewards.

A discrete legal engagement is typically not distributed among many lawyers. The pie is not divided equally. When ten lawyers pitch for the same work, the winner takes all. And to be the winner, you just need to be a little bit better than the competition.

In *Success and Luck*, Robert Frank explained the self-perpetuating effect of winner-take-all markets:

> "Is the Mona Lisa special? Is Kim Kardashian? They're both famous, but sometimes things are famous just for being famous. Although we often try to explain their success by scrutinising their objective

qualities, they are in fact often no more special than many of their less renowned counterparts...Success often results from positive feedback loops that amplify tiny initial variations into enormous differences in final outcomes."

Once a lawyer starts to win new business, they tend to keep winning, just as a best-selling author tends to stay one. With each victory, a lawyer accumulates an advantage over the competition. Assuming they provide high-quality legal services for their client—which is a table-stakes requirement these days—they will have another advocate in the marketplace singing their praises, they will generate positive press, and they will have another success story to add to their website bio. This will make it easier for them to win the next engagement, and so on. The spoils of victory continue to stack up as additional forms of social proof that work in their favor, which keeps the flywheel turning. What starts as a slight advantage over their competition compounds with each subsequent success. As long as they stay focused, they will cement their status at the top of their market. Clients facing serious challenges will begin to seek them out because they want the best lawyer regardless of the cost.

The reasons why some lawyers succeed more than others may seem indiscernible. After all, those at the top aren't necessarily more skilled at the craft of practicing law than their competitors. And most clients can't distinguish between good and great legal work anyway. It's easy to explain away the success of top performers as luck. The truth is, however, that top performers tend to work hard every day to gain an ever-so-slight edge over the competition. The marginal gains they accrue continue to accumulate and compound over time. According to Seth Godin, "With limited time or opportunity to experiment, we intentionally narrow our choices to those at the top."

You may be frustrated about your own lack of business development success at this point in your career, but you should be encouraged by the fact that you don't need to make radical changes or achieve outsized wins to start realizing big rewards. Because you work in a winner-takes-all market, you don't need to work ten times harder to achieve ten times the success. You merely need to start making slight improvements every day that will ultimately compound into huge returns over the course of your career.

To gain your edge, you need to develop the discipline necessary to put the principles discussed in this book into practice every day. Think of the task ahead of you as a 60-minute daily sprint. Just as it is hard to begin a new exercise regimen, your 60-minute daily sprint is going to be difficult at first. Indeed, whenever you're trying to learn something new or develop a new habit, it's a bit of a hard slog at first. Before long, however, as you gain momentum and start racking up some small wins, it will become easier—even enjoyable. You'll develop a business development habit, and the time you carve out for your 60-minute sprint will become an inviolable and energizing part of your daily routine.

There are three components to an effective 60-minute daily sprint that will help you build a successful practice:

1. **Preparation:** You need to plan out how you will use the hour you sell yourself in order to make an impact.

2. **Time Blocking:** You need to schedule and protect your time throughout your day, especially during the first hour of your day.

3. **Pomodoro Technique:** To get the most out of your time, you need to work with intensity and free of distraction.

PREPARATION

———

Over the last decade, Americans have developed a fascination with celebrity chefs, which has led to many chefs becoming pop culture icons. The Netflix documentary series *Chef's Table* has taken the television and cooking worlds by storm since its debut in 2015. It provides viewers with an inside look at some of the world's most renowned chefs and the kitchens in which they operate.

Chef's Table has helped dispel the notion that a successful kitchen is a chaotic one. The stereotype of chefs has long been that they're overworked, overstressed, and lord over their staff members like military dictators. As a result, it's perceived that their kitchens are disorderly and filled with acrimony, marked by clanging pots and pans, salty language, and frenetic energy.

Chef's Table paints a very different picture of what it takes to operate a top kitchen. The best restaurants in the world have kitchens that are orderly—almost serene—and overseen by chefs who exhibit a calm, confident demeanor. In the first episode of season two of *Chef's Table*, chef Grant Achatz and his Chicago-based gastronomy restaurant Alinea are featured. There is a zen-like quality to the kitchen at Alinea, where a 16-to-18 course multi-sensory dining experience for two costs upwards of $700 (without wine pairings).

Achatz learned his trade under the tutelage of Thomas Keller, who is considered by many to be the best chef in America. In 2003 and 2004, Keller's California-based restaurant The French Laundry was named the best restaurant in the world. Achatz spent six years cooking at the French Laundry before moving on to found Alinea.

In his book, *Ad Hoc at Home*, Keller explained that preparation is key to running a successful kitchen:

> "Being organized—as we say in our kitchen, 'working clean'— is a skill to develop. We call it mise-en-place, French for, literally, 'put in place.' The term can be very specific, referring to ingredients needed to complete a recipe, measured out and ready to use, or it can be more general: are you organized, do you have everything you need to accomplish the task at hand?"

"Mise-en-place" is a system chefs use to prepare themselves and their kitchens in the hours leading up to the time meal orders start pouring in. The "Meez," as professionals refer to it, involves studying recipes, making lists of necessary ingredients, measuring proportions and prepping food, and assembling the tools and equipment that will be necessary for cooking that day's menu. Once the preparation is complete, the kitchen is cleaned and reorganized before the real cooking begins. In short, the Meez is the planning phase that allows chefs and their teams to set themselves up for success.

As Anthony Bourdain wrote in his book *Kitchen Confidential,* "Mise-en-place is the religion of all good line cooks… The universe is in order when your station is set…" Accordingly, mise-en-place is as much a mindset as it is a practice; a noun as well as a verb. It's a process that allows great chefs to think ahead, to plan ahead, and to channel their full, undistracted focus to the task at hand.

Lawyers work while sitting at desks, not standing at butcher block countertops, but they, too, can benefit from more structure in their daily routines. Indeed, being productive while engaging in daily business development activity requires daily strategic planning.

BUILD A LIST, BUILD A PRACTICE

When you're idling in rush-hour traffic, an hour seems like a long time. When you sell yourself an hour of your time first thing each morning, it flies right by. The actions you take when you sit down at your desk in the morning will either make or break your business development productivity.

What's the first thing most lawyers do when they get to the office? They open up email, listen to voicemails, and begin tabbing through web browsers—often all at the same time. These types of activities are productivity killers. Some, like web surfing, are distractions that eat away at your time. Others, like checking email, have the potential to entirely disrupt the precious hour you intended to reserve for yourself. The only thing you'll find in an email is a demand or request reflecting someone else's priorities. Those types of distractions can and should wait if you're serious about building a practice. Almost everything you'll find in email can wait for at least an hour.

Instead, start each day with a brief ten-minute planning session—your own Meez. Better yet, plan further in advance. Spend ten minutes at the end of each day planning for the next one. Instead of taking up ten minutes from the hour you sold yourself to focus on business development, get clear on the next day's priorities the evening before. That way you can head home with a clear head, confident that you will be ready to hit the ground running in the morning.

To get in the right state of mind during your planning sessions, begin by reviewing your long-term vision and one-year goals. Not only will this help you plan your day, but it will also allow you to distinguish and prioritize between that which is important and that which is merely urgent. Most importantly, it will enable you to link your daily productivity to a higher purpose.

Once you have taken a moment to focus your mind, create a plan by building a list of actions you will take that day. Building a list enhances execution and improves effectiveness because it helps reduce the urge to multitask and prevents decision fatigue. You can't expect to keep everything straight in your head, so you need to get things down on paper.

While you're going to be focused exclusively on business development for the first hour of your day, I recommend tackling the entirety of your day when building your daily list. Doing so will allow you to purge your brain of mental clutter. By getting your client and administrative work out of your head first thing, you will free up mental space to focus on the task at hand, which, for the next hour, is building a practice. If you're feeling stressed about what you need to accomplish later, you will hinder your ability to optimally perform in the moment.

Making a list may seem like a simple process. It's something you may already do in the course of your day. But not all lists are created equal. Many lawyers' lists resemble something one would use at the grocery store, consisting of 20, 30, or more items with no regard to priority. Occasionally, a lawyer will reshuffle and recompose their running list, and also add to it. Their list doesn't reflect what they will get done on a particular day. Instead, it consists of everything—big, small, important, trivial—that is on their plate.

While it's important to have a handle on the entirety of what you must accomplish, and get it down on paper, a macro-list must be supplemented by a micro-list consisting of a curated collection of the small number of your most important tasks on any given day. Again, getting clear on such priorities requires daily planning and strategic focus. One of the best methods for building such a list was established over 100 years ago.

In 1918, one of the wealthiest and most powerful businessmen in the world went looking for help to improve the efficiency of his managers at Bethlehem Steel Corporation. Charles M. Schwab sought out the assistance of a productivity consultant named Ivy Lee. Schwab invited Lee into his office and, as the story goes, said, "Show me a way to get more things done." Lee responded that all he needed to succeed was to be given 15 minutes with each of Schwab's executives.

Lee spent 15 minutes with each member of Schwab's executive team and handed each a small piece of paper. He then instructed them to do the following:

1. At the end of each day, write down no more than six important tasks that you must accomplish tomorrow.
2. Prioritize those tasks by importance.
3. Upon showing up for work the next day, focus only on the first task. Do not move on to the next task until finishing the first.
4. Proceed through your day in the same manner, one task at a time. At the end of the day, move any tasks that were not completed to a new list of no more than six tasks for the next day.
5. Repeat this process daily.

After three months of implementing these practices, Schwab was so thrilled with the results that he wrote Lee a check in the amount of $25,000—a massive amount in today's dollars. Schwab called Lee's productivity system, which has come to be known as the "Ivy Lee Method," the most profitable business advice he ever received.

The Ivy Lee Method works because it is a structured system, yet simple. It promotes planning, prioritization, and forced discipline, which are all hallmarks of effective productivity. Because it requires that you finish one task before moving on to the next, it also helps cut down on multitasking.

To become more productive throughout your day, it's not essential that you strictly adhere to the Ivy Lee Method, but it is important that you develop some sort of system that incorporates the Ivy Lee principles of planning, prioritization, forced discipline, and single-tasking. By doing so, you'll set yourself up for success each day.

The approach I recommend to my coaching clients builds off the Ivy Lee Method, with one critical distinction to allow for the prioritization of business development activity in a lawyer's daily routine. Here's how it works:

1. **At the end of each day, or first thing in the morning, briefly review your Vision Statement and one-year goals.** This will help to sharpen your focus and allow you to distinguish between the important tasks that will help move you closer to achieving your goals, and those that are merely urgent.

2. **Write down the single business development activity you will engage in during the first hour of your day.** If you're going to write an article, then write. If you're going to send follow-up emails to prospects you met at a networking event last week, send emails. Don't try to do too much in a single day—stay focused on the task at hand. By single-tasking, you'll get in the flow and be more productive. If you try to bounce between tasks, the hour you reserved for business development will result in

only 30 minutes of productivity.

3. **Write down no more than five important tasks that you will accomplish on behalf of your clients that day, and order them in terms of priority, with the most important coming first.** There's nothing magic about the number five. On many days, to the extent possible, you'll be better off working on only one task, such as writing a brief or preparing for an oral argument. Again, productivity suffers when we spread ourselves too thin.

4. **In the first hour of your day, focus only on business development.** Do not move on to client work until the hour you sold yourself ends. To stay on track—and this is important—do not get caught up in your email inbox or listen to voicemail messages until the hour is done.

5. **Once you've moved on to client work, focus only on the first client-related task on your list.** Do not move on to the next task until finishing the first.

6. **Proceed through your day in the same manner, one task at a time.**

7. **At the end of the day, or first thing the next morning, move any tasks that were not completed to a new list of no more than five tasks for the next day.** Even if you left off in the middle of a task, don't pick it back up the next day until after you've completed your daily business development activity.

8. **Repeat this process daily.**

Henry David Thoreau said, "It's not enough to be busy. So are the ants. The question is: What are we busy about?" The system described above will allow you to be "busy about" the most important work that will have the biggest positive impact on your career and enable you to do your best work on behalf of your clients. It will empower you to move through your days with purpose. It's a system for daily action that will steadily move you closer to achieving your goals.

The key to this system is its simplicity. Unlike most lists, which are sprawling aggregations of everything a lawyer has to accomplish without regard to priority, a daily to-do list that identifies one business development activity and no more than five client-related tasks has enough structure to be effective, yet it's simple enough to fit on a 4x6-inch index card. Instead of over-complicating the task of building a list, which can lead to less productivity, it's better to put the minimum amount of effort into a list system that will produce the maximum amount of results. To do this, let's follow the lead of nineteenth-century Italian economist Vilfredo Pareto, whose work has become known as "Pareto's Principle," also referred to as the "80/20 Principle."

The 80/20 Principle stands for the proposition that 80 percent of the benefits that we derive from an activity result from 20 percent of the effort we put into it. Put another way, a few inputs typically lead to an outsized amount of outputs. Pareto developed this insight after observing, year after year, which 20 percent of the pea pods in his garden produced approximately 80 percent of the peas. He then studied and applied the principle more broadly across other areas of economic activity.

You can observe the 80/20 Principle at work in most law firms, where a majority of revenue is generated from approximately 20 percent of clients, and approximately 20 percent of lawyers are typically responsible for bringing in the majority of work. The numbers may vary, so don't get hung up on exact percentages, but the principle remains: Not all activities and investments create equal value. Some are disproportionately valuable.

Since much of what we do matters little, and a small amount of what we do matters greatly, we stand to benefit if we can be more discerning in how we spend our time. When applied to building a to-do list, an 80/20 analysis dictates a simple, scaled-down approach, with a focus on activities that produce the most value.

Whether you adopt the to-do list method described previously or you come up with a method of your own, stay focused on cornerstone principles of daily productivity: planning, prioritization, forced discipline, and single-tasking. By getting things out of your head and down on paper, you'll free up mental capacity to do great work in the moment, instead of always thinking about all the other work you have to do.

There are psychological, as well as productivity, benefits to building lists. Psychologist and author Dr. David Cohen explained, in an article in *The Guardian* newspaper, that list-building helps us to "dampen anxiety" about the busyness and chaos of life and work, gives us structure to our days and a plan to work from, and provides tangible proof of what we have accomplished every day.[21] There is great satisfaction to be derived from crossing out a to-do item when you know you just completed the most important task of your day.

Before we wrap up our discussion about the importance of list-building, I want to warn you about the risks posed by a tool that should enhance productivity but often derails it: your calendar. If you're not diligent and disciplined, your calendar will rob you of the time you intend to spend on business development. Most lawyers' calendars are full of other people's priorities, such as meetings, phone calls, court appearances, and other appointments. They're also randomly organized (an oxymoron that seems appropriate given the subject matter).

There is no methodology, other than the existence of an open block of time, to dictate when or how something should be scheduled. As a result, too many lawyers schedule obligations in a scattershot manner that virtually guarantees they will never get into the flow state necessary to do meaningful, deep work.

This problem is exacerbated by the relatively recent practice that has been adopted by most law firms, and the business world more broadly, whereby colleagues have the ability to view open blocks of time on each other's calendars for the purpose of requesting (in many cases demanding) another person's attendance on a conference call or in a meeting. A calendar "invite" can, of course, be declined, but few ever are, especially when they're received from someone up the chain of command.

There is no perfect solution that will allow you to protect your calendar from other people's intrusions. As a busy lawyer, you will have clients, colleagues, and courts of law that will demand your time on their schedule. During the course of your days, you will have to do the best you can to ward off unwelcome interruptions. It's not feasible to block off big chunks of time every day on your calendar. The nature of your job requires that you make the product you sell—your time—available to other people. But not all of it. It's entirely possible to block off one hour of your time every day—at the same time every day—to focus on business development.

Assuming you will engage in business development activity during the first hour of your morning at work, block that time on your calendar. Others who view your calendar will see that time as blocked for meetings. And you will, in fact, have meetings scheduled—meetings with yourself to work on business development. You will have that time reserved to work on your most important priority.

SPRINT THEN RECOVER, RINSE AND REPEAT

Once you've set your business development priorities, and blocked the time necessary to focus on them, the next step is to get to work. We all have the same 24 hours in the day. The question is: How can we get the most done in the least amount of time?

The Pomodoro Technique is a productivity system developed by Francesco Cirillo. It's a technique based on the "sprint/recover" work philosophy. Cirillo's big insight is that we can be more effective, often in far less time, if we work like sprinters, rather than marathoners. It's important to be patient and circumspect over the long term of your career, while at the same time moving fast during the day-to-day. That's where the Pomodoro Technique comes in. Its basic premise is that, when confronting a large task, you should break the work down into brief, timed intervals (called "Pomodoros"), with short periods for recovery in between. (In case you're wondering, work intervals are called "Pomodoros," after the Italian word for "tomato," because Cirillo used a tomato-shaped timer to track his progress as a university student.)

Here's how it works:

- Pick a task.

- Set a timer for 25 to 40 minutes.

- Work intensely on the task during the interval.

- If a distraction pops into your head, write it down, but immediately get back on task.

- At the end of an interval, get up and take a short break (5 to 10 minutes).
- After four intervals, take a longer break (15 to 30 minutes).
- Sprint and then recover to stay focused on the task at hand and sidestep the distractions that lead to a more scattered approach to your work.

While 25 minutes of work may not seem like much, keep in mind that during these intervals you're supposed to be working intensely. No checking emails. No Internet surfing. No chit-chatting. No distractions. This may differ considerably from the multitasking approach you currently employ, which is why the Pomodoro Technique leads to different (i.e., better) results. By focusing intensely on the task at hand, and shutting out all else, both the quantity and quality of your production during these short intervals will be high.

I recommend implementing a Pomodoro approach to your work throughout the day. At a minimum, try sprinting through the time you devote to business development. You don't need big chunks of time to make significant progress if you're working intensely on the task at hand. In fact, there is evidence to suggest that those who spend long periods of time on a task actually get less done than those who work in short bursts.[22] Working in short, predetermined chunks of time allows you to reframe time as a resource that can work for you, not as something you're constantly running out of.

To get the most out of your morning business development routine, try to complete two 25-minute Pomodoros each morning, with a 10 minute break in between to stretch your legs and freshen up your coffee. Free yourself from as many distractions as possible during this time by turning off email notifications and shutting down web browsers (unless you absolutely need Internet access for research related to business development). Unless you're expecting a critical call, silence your office phone ringer and put your smartphone in a desk drawer and leave it there until the end of your hour. By limiting the possibility of distraction, you will put yourself in a position to work with the purpose and intention necessary and make real progress.

DELEGATE AND ELIMINATE

Up to this point, we have spent a lot of time discussing the distinction between tasks that are urgent and important, and those that are important but not urgent. Those in the former category fall within Quadrant 1 of the Eisenhower Matrix. Quadrant 1 tasks, which typically consist of billable client work, make up the majority of most lawyers' days. Important but not urgent tasks, which live in Quadrant 2, primarily relate to business development and should be completed in the hour of your time that you sell yourself each day.

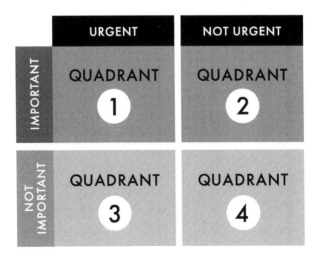

While the tasks that fall within Quadrants 1 and 2 should get almost all of your focus, there is, of course, more on your plate that requires at least some of your attention.

Quadrant 3 includes tasks, generally administrative in nature, that are urgent but not important (at least not relative to client work product and business development), such as logging timekeeping entries, scheduling travel, or communicating with vendors who support your practice. Instead of asking yourself, *Can I do these types of tasks faster?* you should consider whether *you* should be doing them in the first place. If at all possible, delegate Quadrant 3 tasks. We'll discuss how to effectively delegate below.

Everything that falls within Quadrant 4, which includes that which is neither important nor urgent, should be eliminated from your schedule. As Peter Drucker once said, "The biggest waste is doing efficiently what shouldn't be done at all." It's hard to provide a universal definition of what is neither important nor urgent. Much like Justice Potter Stewart's definition of "obscenity," you know it when you see it. But all of us have things we do every day, due to a lack of discipline or out of a sense of obligation, that would be better left undone. Try to eliminate everything that would otherwise fall within Quadrant 4 from your daily routine—more on that in the pages to come.

ENLIST OTHERS IN YOUR PRODUCTIVITY JOURNEY

Given their tendencies toward perfectionism, it's hard for many lawyers to delegate work to others. You've probably had the experience of having too much work on your plate, and contemplated delegating at least some of that work to others, only to find yourself thinking, *It will take more time to delegate this task to someone else, so I might as well do it myself.* We have all been in this position, and it may prove true in the moment—it probably is faster for you to do it yourself. But in the long term, which is what you should be focused on, it's better to get someone else working on tasks that must get done, but not necessarily by you.

For example, let's assume there is a task that is administrative in nature that you must complete every day. This task takes you ten minutes to complete but it would take you ten hours over the course of a few weeks to delegate responsibility for the task to someone else, such as your assistant. While it would be easier and faster for you to complete the task on any given day, by investing ten hours to train your assistant to do it for you, you will start realizing a positive return on that investment within a few months. Not only will you have more time—an hour every week—you will have more mental capacity and clarity as well.

You're one person, undoubtedly a highly capable one, but like all of us you're constrained by the laws of physics. Delegation is one of the few ways to scale yourself beyond your physical constraints—the ability to be in more than one place at one time, the ability to focus on more than one thing at one time—to get more done. Think about it this way: Delegation is a way to buy yourself more time that would otherwise be spent doing mundane tasks, so you can sell yourself more time to focus on things that really matter, like business development.

By learning and practicing the art of delegation, you will be in a position to use your most valuable and finite resource—your time— to your best advantage. Delegation does require you to slow down long enough to get someone else up to speed on what needs to get done, but in the long run, delegation is a catalyst that allows you to operate at your highest potential.

I don't often point to the business practices of doctors as an example of how lawyers should run their own practices, but when it comes to delegation, business-savvy doctors (admittedly, a limited sample size) are doing some things right. Successful doctors, like successful lawyers, sell expertise—not merely their time—so they put in place processes and people that allow them to leverage the amount of expertise they can deliver to each patient in the least amount of time. That's how value is created, and the more value you can deliver in the least amount of time, the more profit you'll generate and autonomy you'll gain.

Think about the last time you visited a well-run medical clinic. At the time you made your appointment, you were probably asked to fill out all of your health history and insurance information in advance. Upon arriving at the clinic, you were greeted by a receptionist who made sure your paperwork was in order. When the time of your appointment arrived (remember, I said "well-run" clinic), you were ushered to your room by a nurse or medical assistant who conducted preliminary diagnostic tests and took notes about any symptoms you were experiencing. Shortly thereafter, the doctor arrived and probably spent 10 or 15 minutes evaluating you before prescribing treatment. Before leaving, you were asked to pay your bill and schedule your next visit. During your hour-long visit to the doctor's office, the doctor may have seen you for 20 percent of the time, and their staff took care of the rest.

You may be thinking, *Well, that sort of delegation may be possible for a visit to a primary care physician for a minor health issue, but it wouldn't be possible for the type of sophisticated legal work that I handle.* That sort of "I can't trust someone else to get this done right" type of thinking is what leads many lawyers to be stressed and overworked because they have a limiting belief that it's not possible to delegate. It is possible but it does require some work.

Even if a task is complex, that shouldn't render it un-delegatable, because every big, complex task is really just a series of smaller ones. Think of any task as part of a hierarchy, with the most challenging, complex parts at the top. Those are the ones you should tackle, and you should try to delegate everything else.

If we shift our focus back to the medical field for just a moment, consider that the most complicated part of health care delivery, which is surgery, includes lots of people performing many functions before the surgeon ever picks up a scalpel. In fact, many surgeries are run according to a checklist—an actual, old-fashioned checklist—that spells out in detail the steps involved in surgery and who is in charge of each step.

The idea of bringing a checklist into surgery was pioneered by Atul Gawande, who is CEO of Haven, the Amazon, Berkshire Hathaway, and JPMorgan Chase-backed health care venture, a globally-recognized surgeon, writer, and public health leader. He is the author of *The Checklist Manifesto*, in which he makes the case that, from operating rooms to airline cockpits, checklists help reduce errors and make professionals better at what they do. As Gawande writes, checklists are there to catch the "stupid stuff" so that professionals can focus on the big stuff.

In his book, Gawande took a look at the legal industry as well, and cites research that found a 36 percent increase in legal malpractice lawsuits over a four-year period were due primarily to administrative mistakes such as missed deadlines. Blown deadlines, filing errors, and other types of "stupid stuff" mistakes could largely be avoided if more lawyers put delegation processes in place that allowed the right people with the right training to handle administrative tasks. Not only does delegation help avoid mistakes, it also allows lawyers to focus on the big stuff, like strategic thinking and business development.

Delegating effectively requires you to work through three challenges: first, how to select the work that can be delegated; second, how to pick the right person to do the work; and third, how to manage the delegation process. The process of delegating can thus be reduced to a Gawande-style checklist, involving the following steps:

Step 1: Sort the tasks that can be delegated. Evaluate the tasks on your plate, particularly those that are recurring, to determine what can and should be delegated.

Step 2: Determine who can work on what types of tasks. Identify people you will rely on, whether inside or outside of your organization, who can take on the tasks specified in the previous step.

Step 3: Create a process. The odds are, because you've done it so frequently, the way you go about completing the task is in your head. Get the process out of your head and down on paper. Create a checklist if possible.

Step 4: Define the task. Precisely define the task, the steps involved, and what is expected in a written document that you provide to the party being delegated to. You cannot expect that the task will be successfully implemented if it is unclear or poorly defined.

Step 5: Transfer the task. Train the person who will now be responsible for the task.

Step 6: Evaluate. Evaluate the implementation of the delegated task and assess how things can be improved.

Step 7: Provide feedback. By evaluating the work, you

will be able to make corrections, if needed, and also provide valuable feedback to the person you have delegated to. Over time, you may find that the person you delegated to is doing the work better than you ever could have done yourself.

If you work at a law firm with lots of internal resources, there is no excuse for not delegating more work to others. When I look back at my time as an associate at a large law firm, I cringe when I think about how little I delegated, and how much easier my life would have been if I had. I shared an assistant with another attorney. There were plenty of paralegals ready to pitch in to help. We had proofreaders, technologists, marketers, and other resources at our disposal. Yet I rarely took advantage of the help that was available..

I fell victim to the *If you want it done right, you better do it yourself* mentality, despite the fact that there were specialists who were better at most things—like proofreading—that I tried to do myself. If I had delegated more, I could have focused more of my time and energy on the things I did best, instead of struggling with tasks I didn't enjoy and wasn't very good at.

If you work at a law firm that doesn't have those types of resources, delegation is still critical, but you may have to invest a bit to get the help you need. If you do, it will be money well spent. From freelancers to virtual assistants, there are people who are great at completing tasks that you don't want to do or shouldn't be doing because your time is best spent elsewhere.

Outside resources can help busy lawyers overcome what researchers call "time famine"—the feeling that arises when you have more work on your plate than time necessary to complete it. Ashley Whillans of the Harvard Business School conducted a study involving thousands of participants in which she studied how people can overcome time famine.

The study concluded that, "Spending money to buy time was linked to greater life satisfaction, and the typical, detrimental effect of time stress on life satisfaction was attenuated among individuals who used money to buy time."[23]

If you're too pressed for time to fit in business development, there's a simple and straightforward solution: Buy back more time by delegating.

ELIMINATE

Warren Buffett once said, "The difference between successful people and really successful people is that really successful people say no to almost everything." One of the primary reasons that gaining autonomy through building a book of business is so important is that it empowers you to say no with greater confidence and frequency.

Even if you don't have clients of your own yet, saying no more frequently is one of the skills you need to develop to get ahead. If you're too busy to take on a new client matter, or non-billable project, say so. The implications of taking on something you can't follow through on will be exponentially worse than any impression created by saying no. Assuming you've established a reputation as someone who comes through whenever possible, a quick and clear no will give the person who was seeking help the opportunity to identify someone else with capacity to do the work. If you say yes but don't have the time to do the work, you'll leave the assigning party with few options with a deadline looming.

If you find yourself with a list of tasks you can't keep up with that are both important and urgent, then you either need to delegate more or you need to establish firmer boundaries by saying no more often. If you don't, then you'll inevitably start cutting into business development time.

However, there are tasks and activities (which fall in Quadrant 4 of the Eisenhower Matrix) that you're undoubtedly spending precious time on at the other end of the important/urgent continuum that you should be saying no to as well. Things you do—and we all do these things—that are neither important or urgent should be eliminated from your to-do list and daily routine altogether. They are merely distractions that must be avoided if you are to have any chance of blocking an hour of time every day for business development activity in the midst of a busy legal practice.

Classifying that which is not important or urgent, and thus should be eliminated, is a subjective determination. Spending 20 minutes every morning perusing *The Wall Street Journal* may be essential to one lawyer, but irrelevant to another. You must honestly and rigorously audit how you spend your time in order to determine what is essential and what can be eliminated.

Start with "low-hanging fruit," such as mindless web surfing (otherwise known as "cyberloafing"), that eats up valuable time and adds little to no value to your day. Work up to saying no to things that may offer more value, such as invitations to lunch from colleagues, but also require big blocks of time. You don't need to, and probably shouldn't, eliminate lunches with colleagues completely, but it's going to be hard to build a practice if you are spending five or six hours a week dining out (unless, of course, you're dining with clients or prospects).

Want to ensure you have enough time to engage in business development activities? Abide by the old adage by working smarter not harder. Don't try to squeeze more into your already over-extended days. Identify that which is wasteful or unnecessary in your daily routine, and steal back that time for what matters most.

REST AND REJUVENATE

Any discussion about productivity, especially as it relates to today's legal profession in which stress and burnout run rampant, is incomplete without addressing the need to rest and recover from the demands of hard work. Yes, one of the effects of productivity is that you'll get more and better work done in the less time. But, no, the purpose of productivity is not to create a vacuum of time that is merely filled with more work.

Throughout this book, I have continually emphasized the idea that you should be thinking about your career with a long-term perspective. That choice was intentional, as short-term thinking and decision-making is what leads many lawyers to fall short of their goals—and many to fall out of the profession altogether.

The key to long-term success is balance. Like a world-class athlete, to be a world-class lawyer you must work intensely and then give your mind and body a chance to re-cover. Type-A personality lawyers feel like they're being lazy when they stop to decompress, but what's lazy is thinking that you can power through any circumstances—including lack of sleep and lots of stress—and expect to perform at a high level.

Top athletes, on the other hand, work in intervals, with bouts of intense training followed by periods of rest and recovery. Building recovery time into training is important because it is during periods of rest that the body adapts to the stress of exercise and grows stronger. Recovery allows the body to replenish energy and repair damaged tissues and muscles. It's when athletes train too hard for too long that they get injured.

The same is true of how you must work as a lawyer. It can't be all intensity all of the time. If your goal is to make partner at a law firm some years from now, look ahead and figure out how to build time for recovery into your schedule. You need to take care of your mind and your body if you want them to function at the peak levels required to be a top performer. When you're working, work hard. When you're not, do your best to detach. Take a long-term approach to your career. If you look at each day in isolation, you'll tend to sprint and burn out. If you have a long-term view, you'll run a slow, methodical marathon and cover much more ground as a result.

It's unrealistic to expect that your life will always be in balance. There will be busy times, and there will be times that are a bit less busy. The key to achieving some semblance of balance is to be thoughtful and purposeful about scheduling time for yourself and for loved ones.

Take vacations to get away, rest, and introduce interesting new stimuli and experiences into your existence. Use flexible schedules to bridge gaps in your career during particularly challenging periods of time in life, such as the birth of a child or when you have to care for a sick parent. It accomplishes nothing—for you, your clients, or your firm—if you continue head down through these challenges while not taking a moment, or even months, if necessary, to decompress and recharge.

One of the principal reasons that it's important to invest an hour of your time each day to focus on business development, is that it helps you ground yourself in the idea that your career is a long-term journey. There's more to the practice of law than billable hours. A myopic focus on billable hours blinds you to the fact that your higher value lies elsewhere—that you can make far more beneficial contributions to your firm, thereby benefiting yourself and those around you. To realize those benefits, however, you must care for yourself so that you have the energy to fulfill your potential.

Just as we know we should be prioritizing business development, but often don't, we know we should be taking better care of ourselves, but rarely do. Again, lack of knowledge is not the issue for most. We know what we should be doing, but the "do-whatever-it-takes" culture of law firm life leads us to push aside our need for more self care. As a result, our desire to work harder leads to diminishing returns and productivity suffers over the long term.

Becoming more productive at business development requires willpower and discipline. It may seem counterintuitive (at least to a non-lawyer), but our personal health and well-being, and therefore our ability to be productive over a longer period of time, does too. So while you're working diligently to build a practice, always keep in mind that your success will be dependent on getting sufficient sleep, eating well, exercising, developing outside interests, and maintaining healthy and fulfilling relationships. In other words, doing all the things you know you should be doing in order to be as productive and effective as possible in your career.

Chapter Summary

———

If you're not consistently doing the work necessary to

build a practice, then it often feels like business development requires a massive amount of effort. However, because you're engaged in a winner-takes-all market, in which those who are marginally better than the competition tend to realize all the rewards, you can achieve a meaningful advantage with small amounts of consistent effort. Just like in the financial markets, the consistent effort you put in will compound over time.

The one hour you sell yourself every day is a sufficient amount of time within which to build a profitable practice, but how you spend your time during your one-hour time blocks is what will ultimately determine your success.

Like the great chefs, you should plan and prepare on a daily basis so that you perform at your highest potential. You must document your plan in writing in the form of an actionable to-do list, with the activities you will engage in during your one-hour business development time block being your first and highest priority. And within that block of time, you must sprint in a straight line, not meander aimlessly, toward your objective. Short, daily sprints, done day after day, will allow you to realize your vision.

To create the space and time necessary to work on business development, you must ruthlessly evaluate the value of each task or project that comes your way. If work has to get done, but not necessarily by you, delegate it. If a task is non-essential, eliminate it from your schedule.

Lastly, the level of success you achieve over the long term is directly proportional to the amount of care and attention you invest into your health and well-being. If you're not caring for yourself, then your productivity will suffer.

COACHING NOTE:
Your Daily To-Do List

Using the guidelines set forth in this chapter, take the time to start planning your days. At the end of your workday, or just before you begin your daily morning sprint, spend ten minutes mapping out your day's tasks. Identify with specificity what you will accomplish during the one hour you're setting aside for business development, and no more than five additional tasks you'll tackle during the remainder of the day. Visit **www.productivitypivot.com** to download the Daily To-Do List template, based on the Ivy Lee Method described in this chapter, to help plan your day.

Get Down to Business (Development)

"Success isn't always about greatness. It's about consistency. Consistent hard work leads to success. Greatness will come."

– DWAYNE JOHNSON

Every day offers a new opportunity to replace bad habits with good ones, to achieve better results than in the past, and to become a more empowered and autonomous lawyer. You're faced with a stark choice: Will you become your most productive self, or will you keep doing things the way you've always done them? As we've previously discussed, the consequences of this choice are significant. Will you choose the more productive path? Will you pivot from your belief that business development is something you merely fit in when you can, and instead start treating it as your most important priority?

Your journey, of course, does not end with you reading this book. It is just beginning. Most people read a book, get inspired in the moment, and then set aside the ideas they learned in search of more inspiration. Being inspired rarely translates into taking action. It's important to make a different choice this time.

It may feel a bit overwhelming to think about the work and discipline required to implement the productivity practices, such as goal-setting and delegation, that we've covered. And if you're feeling that way, it's completely normal. You must face the facts and not assume that there is some quick fix that will allow you to overcome the challenges you face. Hard work will be required.

But consider the alternative. Is the unproductive path any easier? Far from it. In fact, it's much harder to drift through your days, months, and years without any clear plan or purpose guiding your actions, than it is to embrace the challenge.

Now, equipped with your newfound knowledge, it's time to begin. Here is a step-by-step guide that summarizes the key concepts in this book so you can start taking action. Moving forward, use this guide as a reference point as you continue your productivity journey.

1. **Stop and assess.** Set aside some time so you begin focusing on your productivity systems. It's hard for lawyers to hit the pause button, but think about the time you'll spend as a critical investment in your future. The few hours you carve out will pale in comparison to the massive amount of productivity gains you'll realize if you implement only a small amount of the best practices you've learned.

2. **Clarify your vision.** Successful people link their productivity to a higher purpose. You need to clarify your vision of what you want your life and career to be like five or ten years down the road in order to know what steps to take today to move toward your ideal future. Use the Vision Statement template mentioned at the end of chapter 1 to help you think through the critical issues. Finally, keep in mind that your vision for the future may change as your circumstances change. Adjust your vision as appropriate, but only do so after considerable circumspection.

3. **Set goals.** With clear goals in mind, you'll act with more intention and purpose. If you set your goals to align with your long-term vision, and then act accordingly, you'll move forward with greater confidence and success. The most effective way to establish and achieve important goals is by using the SMART goal framework. Establish and write down no more than three SMART goals for yourself using the SMART Goal Worksheet referenced at the end of chapter 2. Revisit your goals frequently to make sure your daily actions are moving you closer to achieving them.

4. **Deconstruct your goals.** Every big goal is made up of a series of smaller ones. To accomplish your long-term goals, you must break them down into a series of small and specific action steps. When it comes to business development, the best way to achieve your goals is to make the activities that drive business development habitual. Business development doesn't happen in one fell swoop—it's the consistency of your effort that matters most.

Small actions, done every day, compound into long-term results. To help break down your goals into specific action steps, use the Weekly Planner mentioned at the end of chapter 3.

5. **Sell yourself one hour every day.** In the practice of law, time is of the essence. Therefore, it's always in short supply. Your time is valuable, and the decision you must grapple with is whether you are going to sell your most valuable time to your clients or to yourself. If you believe the path to a brighter, more autonomous future lies in building a practice, then you should be reserving the first hour of your day, every day, for yourself.

6. **Distinguish between urgent and important.** You could probably spend all day working on urgent client matters if you chose to, but then you would never make any progress on important business development priorities. The Eisenhower Matrix is a tool that helps you think through not only what work you have to do, but also, and more important-ly, what work you should be doing. Use the Eisen-hower Matrix Worksheet referenced in chapter 5 to evaluate whether you're spending your finite time and attention on work that really matters

7. **Make a plan for your day.** If you don't have a plan for each day, then your time will be spent reacting to requests coming your way via email, phone calls, and other inbound inputs. Take control of your day by spending ten minutes at the end of each day or first thing in the morning thinking about how you can deploy your time to achieve maximum impact.

8. **Make a list.** Your daily plan should be documented in a daily to-do list. Creating a list allows you to stay

on track and focus on your most important priorities. Use the Daily To-Do List template referenced at the end of chapter 6 to help plan your days.

9. **Sprint then recover.** Interruptions and distractions can derail your business development progress, so you must resist them as much as possible if you want to build a practice. One of the primary reasons why it's important to tackle business development first thing in the morning is that you will have more willpower to ignore distractions. To stay focused, use the Pomodoro Technique during your business development time. Work intensely, free of distraction, in short bursts. You'll be surprised at how much you can get done during a 25-minute Pomodoro.

10. **Delegate as much as possible.** Consider what work you can delegate, and to whom it can be delegated. It takes time to train someone to do work you've always done yourself, but the investment is worth it. In most cases, even if you spend ten hours training someone else to handle a recurring task, you'll more than make up for that time within a month or two.

11. **Say no.** If you find yourself with a list of tasks you can't keep up with, then you either need to delegate more or you need to establish firmer boundaries by saying no more often. If you don't say no, then you'll inevitably start cutting into business development time. While sometimes you have no choice but to say yes, it's important to start saying no more often.

12. **Rejuvenate.** The purpose of becoming more productive isn't—or at least it shouldn't be—trying to squeeze in more work during the day. Use your newfound productivity to create a well-rounded life. When you're more efficient and effective at work,

it opens up new possibilities to build a rich and rewarding existence outside of the office.

COACHING NOTE:
Take the First Step

Tremendous success is within your grasp. You know what you need to do. You understand what it takes—and what's at stake if you don't take action. You just need to summon the courage and conviction to move forward. Think big about your future. Take the first step. Then another. Nothing, other than your own limiting beliefs about what you are capable of, is standing in the way of you achieving extraordinary results.

Conclusion

A t the age of 38, Geoff Edgers was a reporter for the *Boston Globe*. He was well-regarded and worked at one of the best brand names in the newspaper business, but an unfulfilled professional dream nagged at him. He wanted to make a documentary movie.

Today, in the age of the streaming wars, where companies such as Netflix, Amazon, and Disney are green-lighting more projects than ever, such a dream still seems improbable. In the 1990s, it seemed downright crazy.

Plus, Edgers had a pretty ambitious vision for the movie he wanted to make. He was a fan of the British rock band, The Kinks, and his idea was to try to facilitate the reuniting of the band and film the process.

There were a number of problems with his plan. Edgers knew nothing about making movies. He didn't have any financing. And, as a busy reporter, he lacked time. But that didn't stop him.

Edgers started spending one hour per day working on his movie. A few years later the documentary "Do it Again," which features interviews with Sting, Peter Buck of REM, actress Zooey Deschanel, and other luminaries of the entertainment world, premiered at the International Film Festival in Rotterdam to positive reviews.

In an interview with *Tufts Magazine*, Edgers explained how he pulled it off. "If you wonder whether you could write a book or run a marathon, don't waste a minute calculating your chances," Edgers said. "Instead, spend an hour a day on your dream. It's how I suddenly found myself on a bridge in London, cameras rolling, wondering what took me so long."[24]

All of us have dreams. The difference between people whose dreams remain unfulfilled, and those, like Geoff Edgers, John Grisham, J.K. Rowling, and Charlie Munger, whose dreams have been realized, is that those who succeed set aside the time necessary to make consistent forward progress. Despite their busy schedules, they carve out an hour a day to work on important long-term priorities while still spending the great majority of their time addressing other urgent demands of their careers.

The reason that so many lawyers feel like they lack autonomy in their careers is that they're not investing the time required to acquire the asset—a profitable book of business—that will help them gain more control over their circumstances.

Paradoxically, a lawyer who devotes no time to business development ends up spending far more time on it than those who dedicate an hour a day. That's because all private-practice lawyers know they *should* be spending time developing business. Whether they act on that knowledge or not, it's a task that remains on their mental, if not their physical, to-do lists. Instead of checking it off their lists first thing each morning, and moving confidently forward through their days, it lingers and occupies valuable mental space. Instead of spending just one hour a day on business development, they spend all day on it—they're always thinking about it—because it remains unaddressed.

It's often assumed that stress results from things we do— we do something and then we worry about the outcome. But stress more often stems from things we haven't done. When we put things off, they don't just go away. They fester and remain omnipresent in our minds until they are addressed.

If you've struggled in the past to fit business development into your busy schedule, now is the time to begin anew. The key is simply to get started. What's the next logical action? What's a simple next step you can take to get moving? Once you get started, it's far easier to keep going.

Your long-term objective should be to spend an hour a day on business development. If that seems impossible, then make it easy on yourself by blocking off a mere ten minutes on your calendar each morning. And if you miss a day or two? Don't worry. Just pick up where you left off. Never give up.

Start small, build some momentum, and increase your investment over time. You're trying to build a business development habit, not overwhelm yourself by having your ambition outstrip your capacity. As with any habit, when you start achieving some positive results, you'll naturally start spending more time on the behaviors that are bringing about the results.

Speaking of results, don't fixate too much on them at first. As we've discussed, it takes time to build a book of business. Think of what you're setting out to do as farming not hunting. A farmer must prepare the soil, plant seeds, and nurture them with water and sunlight before reaping a harvest. That's how business development works, too. Developing business is a lagging indicator of the investment you'll be making. The leading indicator is the time you're devoting to the process. If you put in the time, the results will come.

There is no perfect plan. Any type of action, even if it's far from perfect, is better than wasting lots of time planning and equivocating. Getting your mindset right—a mindset that building a profitable practice is possible—is far more important than having a perfect plan. The only way you're going to achieve success is to act, learn from your actions, and then act again. Use a "Ready, fire, aim!" approach. The only mistake you can make is to always fire but never stop to dial-in your aim, or vice versa. Always have a bias toward action. If you do, business development will become a routine part of your day. You'll unlock your highest potential and become an invaluable asset to your firm. Better yet, you'll derive greater satisfaction from your career because you'll be in control of your circumstances.

A bright, profitable, autonomous future in the practice of law is possible. But it's not guaranteed and it won't happen by accident. It's reserved for those who invest the time necessary to build a business development habit—day by day, one hour at a time.

RESOURCES

———

Visit **www.productivitypivot.com** to download the free resources referenced in the "Coaching Notes" at the end of each chapter of this book. These are tools that I use with my coaching clients, and they're available to you for free as a resource to help you achieve higher performance. By downloading these tools, you'll also start receiving my weekly emails in which I share more information about how to build a successful legal practice in the form of articles and podcast episodes I create for my audience.

Several other free resources are available on my website that will help you learn more about what it takes to become a successful lawyer. Visit **www.hcommunications.biz/books** to download:

How to Make an Impact on LinkedIn:
A Step-by-Step Guide for Lawyers
Learn the essential steps to build a network, brand,
and book of business using LinkedIn.

Personal Branding for Lawyers:
Self-Assessment Workbook

Gain a deeper understanding of how to assess your
unique strengths and weaknesses as a lawyer.

ABOUT THE AUTHOR

―

For the last decade, I have devoted myself to helping lawyers and law firms build stronger brands and bigger books of business by providing them consulting and creative services, coaching, and training.

Thought-Leadership Marketing for Lawyers and Law Firms

I am the co-founder and president of Harrington Communications, one of the country's leading PR and marketing agencies for the legal industry. At Harrington, we help lawyers and law firms position themselves as experts and grow their practices through thought-leadership PR and marketing. We provide strategic consulting services and help our clients plan and execute successful thought-leadership initiatives, including content marketing, video, and podcast campaigns. In short, we help those in the legal industry turn expertise into thought leadership, and thought leadership into new business.

Attorney Coaching and Training

I am an executive coach who blends strategic consulting and problem-solving counseling to help lawyers set and reach their business objectives. I work with lawyers in accordance with the principles set forth in this book, for the purpose of building successful practices, including identifying and assessing their goals and then devising strategic action plans to achieve them. As goals are defined, action plans are put in place. My most important job as a coach is to hold clients accountable to the goals they set. Lawyers have the solutions to the challenges they face within them. I simply help them to unlock their potential and set a course for success.

Training for Groups of Attorneys

I specialize in attorney business development training for law firms, both big and small. My training workshops, delivered in-person and virtually, emphasize the importance of smart strategy, action, and accountability, and cover topics related to business development and productivity.

I tailor my training sessions to meet client objectives, and I adjust my approach based on the experience level—from junior associate to senior partner—of my audience. My goal is to leave attorneys educated, energized, and inspired to tackle new challenges.

Interested in working with me and my agency? Learn more about the solutions we provide for lawyers and law firms by contacting me at **jay@hcommunications.biz** or 313-432-0287, or visit my agency website at **www.hcommunications.biz.**

My Background

I am an attorney, author, executive coach and trainer, and marketing consultant. This is my third book. My first book, *One of a Kind: A Proven Path to a Profitable Law Practice*, was published by Attorney at Work in 2016. *The Essential Associate: Step Up, Stand Out, and Rise to the Top as a Young Lawyer* was published in 2018. In addition to my writing and consulting, I frequently speak and conduct training workshops at law firm retreats, bar association gatherings, and other legal industry events.

I live in the beautiful small town of Traverse City, Michigan, with my wife and three young daughters. Outside of work and spending time with family and friends, I enjoy hiking, biking, paddle boarding, golfing, and skiing.

Previously, I was a commercial litigator and corporate bankruptcy attorney at Skadden, Arps, Slate, Meagher & Flom in Chicago, and Foley & Lardner in Detroit. I also co-founded a boutique corporate bankruptcy firm in metro Detroit in 2009.

I earned my law degree from the University of Michigan Law School in 2001, and played baseball (and, yes, studied) at Bowling Green State University. I had the good fortune of competing in the College World Series regional tournament in 1998 (although we were knocked out of the tournament by the number-one ranked University of Miami Hurricanes).

You can read more of my writing at my blog: **www.simplystatedblog.com**. In addition, I encourage you to check out my weekly podcast, The Thought Leadership Project, which you can find at **www.thethoughtleadershipproject.com.** I look forward to continuing this conversation with you!

ACKNOWLEDGMENTS

———

Anyone who has ever tried knows that writing a book is definitely not an individual endeavor. It takes a team to make a book. I am deeply grateful to the people who supported me throughout the process.

Thank you, first and foremost, to my family, including my wife Heather and daughters Madison, Emma, and Kinsey, who supported me during the high points and low ones.

Thank you, as well, to the attorneys, consultants, and other professionals who contributed their insights to the book, and to those who took the time to read manuscript drafts and provided valuable criticism.

I could not have done this without you!

NOTES

Chapter 1

https://www.americanbar.org/groups/lawyer_assistance/research/colap_hazelden_lawyer_study/

https://www.law.com/2019/08/12/by-the-numbers-lawyer-salary-increases-in-the-past-two-decades/

https://www.psychologytoday.com/us/blog/bouncing-back/201106/the-no-1-contributor-happiness

https://ir.law.fsu.edu/cgi/viewcontent.cgi?article=1093&context=articles

https://web.mit.edu/curhan/www/docs/Articles/biases/5_Psychological_Science_33_%28Green%29.pdf

Chapter 2

https://en.wikipedia.org/wiki/Colin_O%27Brady

https://www.amazon.jobs/en/working/working-amazon

https://www.businessinsider.com/jeff-bezos-blue-origin-wings-club-presentation-transcript-2019-2?r=US&IR=T

https://www.dominican.edu/dominicannews/study-highlights-strategies-for-achieving-goals

Chapter 3

https://www.jgrisham.com/bio/

https://www.nytimes.com/2002/09/28/opinion/think-you-have-a-book-in-you-think-again.html

https://news.utexas.edu/2014/05/16/mcraven-urges-gradu-ates-to-find-courage-to-change-the-world/

Chapter 4

https://www.psychologicalscience.org/observer/why-wait-the-science-behind-procrastination

Chapter 5

https://news.stanford.edu/news/2009/august24/multitask-research-study-082409.html

http://discovery.ucl.ac.uk/1465496/

https://www.sciencedirect.com/science/article/abs/pii/S0749597809000399

https://www.pnas.org/content/108/17/6889

https://hbr.org/podcast/2015/03/your-brains-ideal-sched-ule.html

https://journals.sagepub.com/doi/abs/10.1177/1088868307303030

https://journals.physiology.org/doi/full/10.1152/jn.00651.2012

Chapter 6

https://www.theguardian.com/lifeandstyle/2017/may/10/the-psychology-of-the-to-do-list-why-your-brain-loves-ordered-tasks

https://journals.sagepub.com/doizabs/10.1177/0741088397014004001

https://www.pnas.org/content/ealy/2017/07/18/17065411
14

Conclusion

http://news.tufts.edu/magazine/summer2010/planet-tufts/
kinks.html

Made in the USA
Columbia, SC
02 October 2022